The International Interior Design Exhibition

Cover image: Faceted mirror by Jake Phipps

BETA-PLUS

CLASSIC RESIDENCES

Contents

Previous double page: Detail from the Flora table designed by Marcin Rusak represented by Spazio Nobile for the Room by Gert Voorjans at IIDE 2018.

Left page: Master bedroom suite by Carter Tyberghein (detail).

Next double page: The Collectors Gallery at IIDE 2019 designed by Vanessa Bruffaerts. Sculpted polished steel furniture by Pol Quadens, lighting by King's Shops, Paul Smith rug from The Rug Company and artworks by Christopher Coppers.

Beaux Arts
Beaux Arts
Beaux Arts
FIAC 2009
Beaux Arts
Beaux Arts
Beaux Arts
Beaux Arts
Beaux Arts
Beaux Arts
Beaux Arts
SCULPTURE
Beaux Arts
Beaux Arts

Introduction

Having spent the majority of my adult life promoting excellence in interior design, I am delighted to be party to this book, showing interiors created for the exhibitions I have put together over three decades. These exhibitions celebrate the work of highly talented interior designers in carefully conceived rooms, where I would often introduce designers to art dealers and galleries through contacts I had made at Sotheby's and from running a contemporary art gallery in St. James's. The concept was to show high level designed rooms complete with works of art as completely balanced rooms full of ideas and inspiration.

In hindsight, the 1980's became known as the 'designer decade', but in those early days London was a very different place. The city was tired and run-down, with slow economic growth, public buildings blackened with pollution. The great regeneration plan that transformed the docklands and vanished industry, was yet to come. The World of Interiors magazine made its debut in 1982 into a market starved of design magazines and public interest.

My drive has always been to help talent at all levels thrive rather than strive. The exhibitions offer a platform for design excellence without client restraints. I particularly enjoy introducing all manner of creative craftsmen to promote the cross-fertilisation of ideas, exploring haute couture design, ready to influence the way we live. Shabby Chic was encapsulated by Monica Apponyi at BIDE 1991, an exhibition I staged at the *D & D Building*, which I created with Robin Guild at his building in Pimlico as the prelude to *The Chelsea Design Centre*, where I was instrumental in bringing industry support. Ralph Laurent launched their interior design debut at BIDE 1991, the MD coming over to secure a space, where Robin Guild recommended that rooms work best with a fireplace, which was all important to their 'Club' feel. In 1988, architects Mercier - London used plumbers piping to great effect as architraves and dado with black fabric stretched on the walls to achieve a good acoustic with hoof feet furniture by Ron Arad.

The spaces we inhabit reflect who we are, interior designers creating individual environments conducive to the way we feel and interact with each other. My exhibitions have inspired visitors with interior compositions incorporating contemporary sculpture and art set off by carefully designed lighting, sumptuous fabrics, wallpapers and soft furnishings. This visual education, reaches higher levels of understanding lifestyle choices, influencing colour combinations, furniture layouts and innovative design in various guises and styles. Some of us like to live with colour, texture and pattern, others not. Design is highly personal and individual, interior designers leading the way to greater possibilities for our wellbeing and potential.

Moving the exhibition to Brussels as *The International Interior Design Exhibition (IIDE)*, Brussels in the Centre of Europe had exciting prospects, not least to encourage art collectors to create interior around their collections.

My thanks to Wim Pauwels of Beta-Plus Publishing for celebrating the creative efforts of the designers, suppliers and craftsmen that I have had the pleasure to work with, with special emphasis on the designers who exhibited over the past two years in Belgium.

IIDE:
a brief history 1982-1997

First launched in London by Fleur Rossdale as *The British Interior Design Exhibition (BIDE)* during the 1980's & 1990's, the event was highly acclaimed as a ground-breaking showcase for the design industry. With 30,000 international visitors to each, the exhibition helped propel interior design into the limelight, receiving worldwide press coverage and an insatiable demographic of private clients, hoteliers, designers and developers, interiors on show stretching their imagination.

Fleur was excited to establish the BIDE as Europe's first high end interior design exhibition, which welcomed the public as well as "The Trade". Interior designers were selected with careful curation by Fleur to showcase their skilled and diverse palate of soft furnishings, lighting, works of art and fine furniture as perfectly balanced rooms. The exhibition inspired visitors to either purchase art and decorative pieces, take away ideas or engage the designers.

The exhibitions helped change perceptions, visitors understanding that working with professionals saved both time and costs. The pioneering mix of design with fine art over a 15-year period of the exhibitions helped fuel the return to the quality of design that had arrived in London from the US with the establishment of Colefax & Fowler in the early 20th Century. BIDE forged to re-establish the relationship between interior designers and fine art, investment in property and aesthetics going hand in hand.

In 1991, Fleur staged "Interiors by Couturiers", including Vivienne Westwood, Amanda Wakely, Victor Edelstein and Bruce Oldfield, which was well-received by both press and public visitors.

Fleur chose to re-launch her exhibition in Brussels to bring international design ideas to the capital of Europe, honouring a rich Belgian cultural heritage in design and also its sense of surrealism, the exhibition a mix of fact and fantasy. The founders of the highly decorative Art Nouveau movement, led by Victor Horta and Henry van der Velde, they in turn were influenced by Arts & Crafts, which emerged from Japan developed by Carl Larsson in Sweden and William Morris in the UK in the mid- 19th Century. Post-war austerity meant that Art Nouveau was no longer affordable nor fashionable and Horta led the way to Art Deco. Henry van de Velde was instrumental in the creation of the Bauhaus in Germany and La Cambre in Brussels in the late 1920s. His house De Bloemenwerf in Brussels is emblematic of van de Velde's vision of interiors as a complete work of art. 'Decoration is all about a skilled designer bringing together specialist workmanship, colour, texture and fine art to create a melodious interior to enhance our everyday lives', says Fleur.

British Interior Design
1982
Interiors by nine celebrated Interior Decorators and Designers in one of the finest houses in Regent's Park:
Bill Bennette Design Ltd · Dargie Lewis Designs Ltd
Fox Linton Associates Ltd · Charles Hammond Ltd
Herbert Nevile Ltd · Samuel & Cooper Ltd
Simon Playle Ltd · John Siddeley International Ltd
George Spencer Decorations Ltd
The exhibition includes Fine Paintings, Sculpture, Antique and Modern Furniture from leading galleries and features many new fabrics, wallcoverings and carpets.
Entry by catalogue available at £2.50 (inc p&p) from:
ART & DESIGN PROMOTIONS LTD
25 Bedford Row London WC1R 4HN
Telephone: 01 242 6171
OPEN ON THURSDAYS AND FRIDAYS FROM 12·00 MIDDAY TO 7·30 PM AND ON SATURDAYS FROM 12·00 MIDDAY TO 5·00 PM
2ND SEPTEMBER TO 2ND OCTOBER 1982

BIDE edition 1 (1982)

1 Cornwall Terrace, Regent's Park, London

A selection of press cuttings from The British Interior Design Exhibition 1982 (BIDE). Exhibitors included Fox Linton Associates; John Siddeley International, Simon Playle Limited, George Cooper as Samuel & Cooper, Charles Hammond, George Spencer Decorations, Bill Bennette Design, Herbert Nevile, Dargie Lewis Designs, Siddeley Landscapes, Galleria Monte Carlo with catering by The Admirable Crichton. Fleur launched David Linley as his agent, who created an Olé Chet in sycamore with leather door covering working with Derek Frost for Fox Linton.

Introduction

British Interior Design 1982

As you enter 1 Cornwall Terrace to view the exhibition 'British Interior Design, 1982' we trust that you will be impressed by the interior and the special atmosphere which has been created in this beautiful Nash house.

Nine interior designers, ranging from the best known Knightsbridge companies to younger individual designers: Bill Bennette Design Ltd; Dargie Lewis Ltd; Fox Linton Associates; Charles Hammond Ltd; Herbert, Nevile Ltd; Simon Playle Ltd; Samuel & Cooper Ltd; John Siddeley International Ltd., and George Spencer Decorations Ltd., were invited to the house in March to look at the empty shell. Each of them had free range in selecting an area in which they could express their idea of interior design. Plans were drawn up, and the designers consulted each other in order to achieve an overall harmony in the house, whilst retaining an individual character for each room. Wit, craftsmanship and daring played their part, together with taste, tradition and harmony, and each designer created interiors representative of his particular style, philosophy and personality. We consulted the designers on the choice of paintings, furniture and fine art; leading galleries have kindly loaned works of art and furniture as part of the exhibition.

From June to August the house was alive with builders and craftsmen; the designers were busily supervising all the details that are so important if a perfect finish is to be achieved.

The results are, as you will see, imaginative, stimulating and always beautiful. In the following pages the individual designers explain how they approached the decoration of each room, the careful attention that they gave to choosing lighting and works of art and how in some cases they designed special fabrics and wall-coverings for the exhibition.

We would like to express our thanks to all the designers, suppliers and dealers for their enthusiasm and support. Our thanks also go to Lord Kenilworth for creating a beautiful garden, and to Viscount Linley and Margaret Martin who have made or designed pieces of furniture expecially for the exhibition.

Art & Design Promotions Ltd
25 Bedford Row
London WC1R 4HN
Tel: 01-242 6171

Fleur Rossdale
Fleur Rossdale

Ian Thompson
Ian Thompson

and **right** *Two views of the ...elevision room, designed by ...ddeley International. The two ...he room cleverly juxtapose ... and grey colour-scheme. The ...et (by BIC), marblised dado ...ce link both areas. The faux ...neo-classical bookcase was ... Cupboard Love; the vinyl ...ring is by Lines of Pinner.*

...ion was carried out by ... Horner.

...first area, the staircase-...s decorated by Fox Lin-...ociates. The aim was to ...m the space into a gallery ...ollector of contemporary ...s, a series of cool greys ...een as a discreet foil for ...s and sculpture.

...e left of the hall is the ...elevision room by John ... International. Chief ..., Paul Gilbert, was anx-... to produce too tradition-...k and this area of the ...was well-suited to the ...contemporary setting he ...mind. The shape of the

Cornwall Terrace & The Picturesque   *Fore...*

ANTHONY MOULD

As the illustration shows so clearly, little has changed to the exterior appearance of 1 Cornwall Terrace, last of nineteen adjoining houses at the south westerly point of the Regent's Park development. Designed and built by James and Decimus Burton in 1821 under the supervision of John Nash, architect to the Prince Regent, with its handsome bow window, satyr caryatids and great free standing columns, it remains among the most impressive productions of this team. Its enclosed garden was exposed to particular regulations by Nash himself, yet further plans for wooded gardens along the south side were vetoed for fear that the distant aspect be marred.

These villas must of course be seen within the context of the overall development, an exercise in the Urban Picturesque which, at the turn of 1800, was the most avant-garde architectural thinking in this country. Following from the theories of men such as Richard Page Knight, William Gilpin and Uvedale Price, a new attitude to nature, to landscape gardening and in turn to architecture within landscape was evolving. As had been achieved at Downton Castle in Herefordshire, architects now sought to combine the irregular silhouettes of their houses with th... requirements of mo... domesticity. There ... better exponent of ... new ideas than John...

While some of th... measurements and ... detailing in his worl... be erratic, his broad ... genius remains beyo... doubt, to our own ... to those of his contemporaries'. His collaboration with Humphrey Repton, the landscape designer, was over by 1802, but the lessons learnt are clearly to be seen in the Regent's Park development as it took shape in 1810. This was to be an independent urban unit giving provision for all classes of the community; that Nash may have drawn some inspiration from Claude Nicholas Ledoux's designs for the town of Chaux near Besancon is not ... so many directions, Nash seems to have been strangely neglectful of applying his talents to the inside as well as to the outside of his villas.

The house is divided into nine sections, each of which has been decorated by a different designer. Never before on such a scale under the same roof can so many different skills have been combined. Sculptors, painters and art dealers have contributed to provide works of many contrasting styles and periods. Nash houses are

Detail of mansion in CORNWALL TERRACE 1828 Crace Collection British Museum

I gives me great pleasure to write about a dream of a Nash house, magnificent in every aspect, which has come to my attention. This low built mansion enjoys exquisite views over Regents Park with its 300 acres of lakes, tennis courts and parkland. The house itself has one of the largest private gardens in Regents Park and, surrounded by 150 Cyprus trees, complete seclusion and privacy are ensured. The fountains, the gazebo and rock gardens add to the picture...

I was fascinated to discover that the house was almost entirely reconstructed and restored to its former grandeur, retaining the original Nash facade. It was through the vision of a gifted, young Fine Art & Interior Design consultant FLEUR ROSSDALE who, with the wholehearted cooperation of the owner, enlisted the talents of some of Britain's top designers fully to develop the potential of one of London's finest houses.

The end result was so spectacular that a series of glittering society parties were given in celebration! Amongst the many distinguished guests were The HON ANGUS OGILVY and HRH PRINCESS MARGARET. (Charles Hammond Limited who designed the drawing room were so delighted with it that they obtained the owner's permission to celebrate the firm's 75th anniversary with a gala party in that very room).

I enjoyed wandering through this gracious family home and after seeing half a dozen fabulous bedroom suites, I lost count. Looking out of the bow window in the drawing room on the first floor, with Regents Park extending on my right and the floodlit garden before me I found it difficult to believe I was in the heart of central London.

I am told that the numerous security systems will ensure the peace of mind of the family. The automatic gates open onto a sweeping carriage driveway with ample parking and garage space for several cars. Besides the main house, which even includes a passenger lift, there is spacious staff accommodation as well as a charming adjoining mews house.

I have reason to believe that this property may be for sale, in the region of £4 million. What a marvellous opportunity to acquire what may be the finest private house in London!

PRESS CUTTINGS

COUNTRY LIFE—AUGUST 19, 1982

British Interior Design 1982

Interiors by nine celebrated Interior Decorators and Designers in one of the finest houses in Regent's Park:

Bill Bennette Design Ltd · Dargie Lewis Designs Ltd
Fox Linton Associates Ltd · Charles Hammond Ltd
Herbert Nevile Ltd · Samuel & Cooper Ltd
Simon Playle Ltd · John Siddeley International Ltd
George Spencer Decorations Ltd

The exhibition includes Fine Paintings, Sculpture, Antique and Modern Furniture from leading galleries and features many new fabrics, wallcoverings and carpets.

Entry by catalogue available at £2.50 (inc p&p) from:

ART & DESIGN PROMOTIONS LTD
25 Bedford Row London WC1R 4HN
Telephone 01 242 6171

OPEN ON THURSDAYS AND FRIDAYS FROM 12·00 MIDDAY TO 7·30 PM AND ON SATURDAYS FROM 12·00 MIDDAY TO 5·00 PM
2ND SEPTEMBER TO 2ND OCTOBER 1982

RECEPTI...

Bedroom & Bathroom Three

HERBERT, NEVILE LTD
20 Lennox Gardens
London SW1
Tel: 01-584 3073

Herbert, Nevile Limited was formed three years ago when both partners decided that their mutual talents would successfully combine to form a base for an Interior Design Company.

Nick Herbert spent several years working for a leading Interior Decorating firm and Christopher Nevile had had a very successful career with a top advertising and design consultancy.

They have gathered together a team of assistants who, like themselves, have worked in established decorating businesses.

Herbert, Nevile consider that it is always a good idea to start at the top and better still to stay there. The rooms at the top of 1 Cornwall Terrace have been created to show the best in traditional design, with all the comfort and ease necessary for modern living. The setting is ideal for a peaceful and light attic bedroom. The fabric chosen for the windows, bedspread and sofa is a hand blocked French cotton in soft pinks and blues which is complimented by plain linen used on the chairs, bedhead and table cloth.

The walls are painted in trompe l'oeil panels of off-white and blue. The lighting is understated and the pictures, antiques and other decorative pieces have been chosen and arranged with care.

The overall effect is not so much a show, more of a simple and pretty room:- the kind of room in which one could so easily live.

DESK Early 19th century French desk with marbled top.

PICTURE 'Shootr-Suwar, or Camel Messenger,' hand coloured lithograph after Emily Eden, 1844. From Portraits of the Princes and Peoples of India from Eyre and Hobhouse Limited

Suppliers

QUILTED FABRICS: Bedhead, Quilted Bedspread, Bed Valance, Skirted Table, Bedside Tables: all by Cover Up Designs

CARPET: Pin Dot from Benardout of Chelsea

RUG: Dhurrie from the Rug Shop

CURTAINS: French handblocked chintz available from Herbert, Nevile Ltd.

UPRIGHT CHAIRS: Designed by Herbert, Nevile Ltd. made by The Norfolk Furniture Company Ltd.

ANTIQUES: Ning

PICTURES: Eyre and Hobhouse Limited

CANAPE: Herbert Nevile Ltd.

COFFEE TABLE: Faux Bois

SPECIAL EFFECTS: Trompe l'oeil panelling and marbling in Bathroom by Faux Bois

Fabrics and carpets protected by Fiber-Seal

CARPET Pin-Dot design from Benardout of Chelsea.

FABRIC French handblocked chintz from Herbert, Nevile Ltd.

SIMON PLAYLE LIMITED
420 Fulham Palace Road,
London SW6 6HY
Tel: 01-385 3910

Simon Playle has been a professional interior decorator for over ten years and established his own business three years ago. His work includes houses, flats and offices both here, in America and the Far East. As a supplier of exclusive handprinted American fabrics and wallpapers Simon Playle was invited to participate in the Designers Showhouse scheme.

He realised that this would be the perfect opportunity to use the latest and most beautiful designs available in a room which he felt would show them to their best advantage.

The Olan wallpaper designed by Charles Tausch for The Twigs in Boston has never been seen in Europe until now and is unique in that it is the twentieth century equivalent of the French eighteenth century 'papiers peints' which were used extensively, and with such effect, in the chateaux of France during the 'age d'or'. Olan has complementary dado and sidewall papers, the former hung horizontally and the latter vertically which creates the room's magical arboreal atmosphere.

Simon Playle feels very strongly that curtains are an item in a room that must never be neglected. They are tremendously important, not only for day to day practicality but also because they furnish and finish a room. Take them down and the room is bare.

The chic contrast provided by the curtains used here serves only to ... was made impossible by fitting a wall-to-wall carpet so instead chose to use a carpet, made by Bosanquet Ives, which can easily be taken up from the bleached wood floor.

Due to the pace of life today it is all too easy for things to have a functional purpose; because of this Simon Playle has tried to recapture in the dining room some of the elegance, fun and frivolity of the past through the use of modern fabrics and traditional techniques to give us the best of both worlds.

Suppliers

...PAPER 'Olan' Handprinted and available in seven col...

...: 'Reef' 100% glazed cotton ...e available in seven ...ways.

UPHOLSTERY 'Beneze... available in ten colo...

Bedroom Four

DARGIE LEWIS DESIGNS LIMITED
40 Kings Road,
London SW3 4UD
Tel: 01-589 5956

Lavinia Dargie IDDA started her own design business six years ago. The business is kept small and personal so that great attention can be made to individual client requirements. Most of the work undertaken is in the domestic field in London and the country with occasional work abroad.

This bedroom posed a pair of immediate and daunting problems in that both windows, one a dormer, are set very high with large expanses of wall beneath. The dormer window accentuates the problem by opening inwards precluding the use of any form of blind and full length curtains have therefore been designed to hang from the ceiling at the front of the sloping soffits and are held back by a fabric covered batten. Full length curtains have also been used on the other window but here a festoon blind has been added to conceal the deadlight above the window and a serpentine shaped cover has been made to house a radiator below and to display a mid-nineteenth century bust.

Once these initial hurdles had been overcome a chintz was chosen from a new collection and the soft contours in the design have been reflected in the shape of the bedhead and in the quilting of the bedspread.

Simple matting was selected as floor covering and a late nineteenth century dhurrie in a lovely spacious design was found to complete the scheme.

RUG Room Dhurrie, c. 1910, 8' 5" × 6' 6" (2.57m. × 1.99m.). Courtesy of David Black Oriental Carpets.

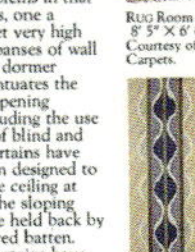

FABRIC 'Harlequin' printed satin, 137cm. wide by Pallu & Lake.

LAMP Chapman Lamp. Cut corner urn with handles. Antique brass finish with Havana leather. 28" high. Courtesy of Baker Knapp & Tubbs ref: E 54004 A21.

PAINTING 2nd Duke of Wellington, thought to be in the attire of the order of St. Patrick, c. 1820. Pencil & watercolour on prepared paper by Richard Cosway, R.A., 12" × 8". Courtesy of Anthony Mould Ltd.

Suppliers

RUG: David Black Oriental Carpets

FRESH FLOWERS & PLANTS: Pulbrook & Gould Limited

DECORATIVE FLORAL EFFECTS: Kenneth Turner Flowers Limited

OBJECTS D'ART: Portmeirion Antiques

PICTURE FRAMING: P. R. Elletson & Co.

CARPET: B & T Carpet Planners

FABRICS: Pallu and Lake

UPHOLSTERED FURNITURE: L M Kingcome Limited

LIGHTING & FURNITURE: Baker Knapp & Tubbs Limited

Above *The fabrics and wallcovering in the dining-room are all from Simon Playle. The scheme has a pleasing touch of fantasy, heightened by the flamboyant curtaining. The antique furniture is from W R Harvey and Mallett at Bourdon House; the flowers are from Kenneth Turner.* **Left** *Looking from the staircase-hall to the library/television room.*

in the project were Bill Bennette; Dargie Lewis; Fox Linton Associates; Charles Hammond; Herbert, Nevile; Simon Playle; Samuel & Cooper; John Siddeley International; and George Spencer. Each chose a room in which to exercise personal skills. Not only did the designers evolve total schemes for the rooms, but chose all accessories, including paintings and decorative objects. One characteristic evident throughout the house is the high standard of craftsmanship, especially in the use of decorative finishes, such as the marbled walls and grained woodwork. Much of the building work and

▲ غرفة طعام صغيرة تسمى غرفة الافطار تستعمل لتناول وجبات الاسرة يومياً. من تصميم جورج كوبر

◀ غرفة نوم من تصميم جورجينا توك .

ANTIQUE COLLECTOR
DEBORAH STRATTON
SEPTEMBER 1982
Inside THE Trade
ANTIQUE COLLECTOR'S MONTHLY LOOK AT THE ART & ANTIQUES TRADE
British Interior Design Takes Off
Bedroom Two
GEORGE SPENCER DECORATIONS LIMITED
At home with the designers
BY ELIZABETH WILLIAMSON
POINT DE VUE IMAGES DU MONDE
LA SEMAINE DES ALTESSES
TH SEPTEMBER
Inside BELGRAVIA
British Interior Desig
Show-house showcase
A mass of publicity has attended the refurbishing of what is being called 'the most beautiful house in London', 1 Cornwall Terrace, London NW1.
Harpers & Queen
OMES IN A LLION
ine interior designers embellish No 1
£4,000,000 buys No 1, Cornwall Terrace, NW1 (top). Fleur Rosedale (above), in the drawing room with a client)

THE
BRITISH INTERIOR DESIGN
EXHIBITION 1988
26TH MAY- 19TH JUNE 1988
AT
THE CHELSEA OLD TOWN HALL, KING'S ROAD, LONDON SW3
Complete room sets by leading interior designers with:
New Fabrics • Books • Furniture • Lights and Lighting • Accessories • Paintings and Antiques • All items for sale
OPENING HOURS
Monday to Friday 11.00 am to 7.00 pm Wednesdays 11.00 am to 8.00 pm
Saturdays and Sundays 11.00 am to 5.00 pm
ADMISSION
£6.00 including Catalogue, reductions for Students, OAP's, Children and Groups
Further information is available from:
The Interior Design House Ltd • 3 Pembroke Square • London W8 6PA • Tel. 01 938 4759

BIDE edition 2 (1988)

Chelsea Old Town Hall, Chelsea London

A selection of press cuttings from The British Interior Design Exhibition 1988 (BIDE). Exhibitors included: Parish-Hadley Associates, Parke Interiors, Machin Designs, David Hicks International, Borland Interiors, Blasé Design, Bennison, Rory Ramsden, Woodstock Designs, Spencer-Churchill Designs, Gordon Lindsay, Mercier - London, Anna Tatham, Thorp & May, Anthony Paine, Wiltshire Interiors, Alidad Limited, Beckett & Graham with David Linley, Jonathan Hudson Interior Decorations, Indiaworks by Robin Guild, Sudeley Design, Joanna Trading, Christopher Nevile Design Partnership, Simon Playle Limited, Rossie Designs, Ian G. Shaw and The Chelsea Gardener. A colonnade within the fabric of the building showed supplier rooms by Manuel Canovas, House & Garden Magazine, Inchbald School of Design, Osborne & Little, I.S.I.D and David Linley Furniture.

HER MAJESTY'S CONSULS LIST
April/May 1988 No. 897
The International Diplomatic and Consular Reference Directory Since 1903
Every room tells a story at the British Interior Design Exhibition
Interior design first for London
HOUSE BEAUTIFUL
OCTOBER 1988 $1.95
HB TODAY
ENGLISH STYLE GETS PARED DOWN AT BRITAIN'S FIRST MAJOR SHOWHOUSE
LONDON'S LATEST
HOUSE & GARDEN
INCORPORATING WINE & FOOD MAGAZINE
Worldscope
TIME FOR EXHIBITIONS
Trade Review
LONDON IN JUNE
The art of design
PRIVATE VIEWS
Today's royal engagements
LONDON DIARY
Big launch for design exhibition
THE TIMES
WEDNESDAY MAY 25 1988
Decorati
ANTIQUE DEALER AND COLLECTORS GUIDE
OCTOBER 1988
THE ART OF ELEGANCE
LONDON LOG
Interior design first for London
A SMILE
THE CONSERVATORY PARTY
BRITISH INTERIOR DESIGN SETS THE STYLE

Harpers & Queen
JUNE 1988

ROLL CALL

CONNOISSEUR
JUNE 1988 $3.00
THE GUIDE TO THE CIVILIZED WORLD

INTERIOR MINISTERS GATHER

CONNOISSEUR'S WORLD

Chelsea floor show

LIVING

Woodentoff

Not just talented, not just professional, not just royalty

Gill Martin talks to Lord Linley, Steve Wood took the pictures

'I'm not trying to be modern, clever or tricky'

tektur ohnen

Aktuell: Möbel-Show in Chelsea

OUT & ABOUT

INSIGNIA
MAGAZINE

SUNDAY TELEGRAPH
No. 1411 JUNE 5, 1988 Price 45p

COLLECTING
A Fair cop
Deborah Stratton

TRADITIONAL INTERIOR DECORATION

HOUSE & GARDEN

Classical bathroom

Inspired by Biedermeier and Regency; photographed by Peter Warner

PUBLIC EYE
PAUL BARKER

Roll on the revolution

Imitated

Design show

Pony for Princess Margaret

BRITISH INTERIOR DESIGN EXHIBITION

EXHIBITIONS & ART
SPECIAL SHOWS

BIDE edition 3 (1989)

Chelsea Old Town Hall, Chelsea London

A selection of press cuttings from The British Interior Design Exhibition 1989 (BIDE). Exhibitors included: Bonetti & Garouste, Designers Guild, Blasé Designs, Rory Ramsden, George Spencer Designs, Scarisbrick & Bate, Nicholas Glover Associates, Fox Lindon Associates, Beaudesert, David Hicks International, Mercier - London, Jameson Designs, Meltons, Pawson Silvestrin, Rosemary O de C Hamilton, Morrow Reis Designs, Robina Cayzer, Alidad Limited, MC Squared, Parke Interiors, Broosk Interior Design, The Royal College of Art, Ian G. Shaw, Christopher Nevile Design Partnership and Helen Cooper Associates and Pimlico Print Rooms. A colonnade within the fabric of the building showed supplier rooms by Manuel Canovas, House & Garden Magazine and Traditional Interior Decoration Magazine, National Trust and Christie's.

Harpers & Queen
THE WILDER SHORES OF PARIS
The Daily Telegraph
IN SHORT
WEDNESDAY, MAY 3, 1989
COLLECTOR
The British Interior Design Exhibition
HOMEWORK
DESIGNERS GUILD
COUNTRY LIVING
JUNE 1989
THE DESIGNER'S EYE
HOMEWORK
HOMEWORK
CHRISTIE'S
International Magazine
British Interior Design Exhibition
by Paul Atterbury
PUBLIC VIEWS
INTERIOR
DECORATION
A CONTRAST OF INTERESTS
Jo Newson anticipates minimalist and traditional styles at the British Interior Design Exhibition this summer

ROOM
READING
HELEN
COOPER
WOMAN'S JOURNAL
TONIGHT'S WEATHER: SULTRY
LATE PRICES EXTRA
Evening Standard
LONDON, WEDNESDAY, 24 MAY, 1989
DESIGN
Designs on nature
Linley backs the classics
The Daily Telegraph
FRIDAY MAY 19, 1989
PETERBOROUGH
Fashion victim
OBSERVER IN LONDON
21 MAY 1989
T
25 Thursday
HOUSE & GARDEN
INCORPORATING WINE & FOOD MAGAZINE
PUBLIC VIEWS
Exhibitionism
The British Interior Design Exhibition is imperative viewing for everyone interested in decoration. Some of the exhibitors' rooms are seen here in artists' impressions
ONE IN VERMILION
Some say that chintz is dead—while others just break all the rules. The new interior design star Alidad does precisely that. Criminal? Journal's June Ducas followed a hunch at this year's British Interior Design Exhibition, picked up a few clues and turned sleuth to make this study in scarlet
THE WORLD OF INTERIORS
ANTENNAE
What's in the air this month, edited by Ros Byam Shaw
PUBLIC VIEWS
PUBLIC VIEWS
HAMMERSMITH AND FULHAM TIMES
From high tech to tassels . . .
By BARBARA DENNY
STEALING THE SHOW
DESIGNS FOR LIVING OR NOSTALGIA TRIP?

BIDE edition 4 (1990)

Chelsea Old Town Hall, Chelsea London

A selection of press cuttings from The British Interior Design Exhibition 1990 (BIDE). Exhibitors included: David Hicks International, Harrods with David Linley for Harrods, Joanna Trading, Christopher Nevile Design Partnership, Nicolas Glover Associates, MM Design, Anthony Paine Limited, Christophe Gollut, Nick Allen Consultancy, Kensington Designs, Charles Rutherfoord & Nobby Clarke, Broosk Interior Designs, Miriam Cobrin Designs, Derek Frost Associates, Jenny Armit Interiors, Pavillion Designs, Melissa Wyndham Limited, Smallbone & CO of Devizes, Suddeley Castle Furniture and Paula Durante Interiors. A colonnade within the fabric of the building showed supplier rooms by Clare Mosley, O'Shea Gallery, The Chelsea Gardener, House & Garden Magazine, Martin Robinson Flowers, Angus Gibson Music, Kevin McCloud, Rivière Furniture,

The Magazine, April '90

The Inside Job

Helene van der Ploeg creates an ideal home

Imagine a family. Richard is making a name for himself in the City. Elizabeth is coping with two teenage daughters, a baby boy and a hectic domestic and social life. Richard has recently been promoted and they are all set to move into a larger house more suited to their needs. Although much work needs to be carried out, they are able to make their new home individual and unique with the help of a few well-chosen companies.

Their first port of call is **George Spencer Designs Ltd.** They want to construct designs around ideas they already have and therefore they need a company who will be able to convert their needs into reality with the minimum of fuss. George Spencer Designs offer a full interior design service where quality and customer care are of paramount importance. Although their designs are unmistakably classic, ...

... window seats.

For the sitting-room Richard chooses the Howard-style sofa with its ample cushions and deep back which make it perfect for flopping into at the end of a hard day's work. Combined with the Victorian stools and a beautifully woven Turkish kilim suspended from the wall this is style indeed!

In both the drawing-room and the sitting-room the focal points are the huge open fireplaces. As it is an area where everyone comes together it needs to be highlighted with dramatic effect. Mirrors are the answer.

It is becoming increasingly difficult to find old overmantel mirrors with the right dimensions and price-tag. The specialist company to visit is **Overmantels** in Highgate. Used skilfully, mirrors are capable of creating an extra dimension and providing a beautiful area of interest.

Room for views: George Spencer Designs Ltd.

Kilim collectables from David Seyfried

Below: 'The Cellar' by Jenny Armit Interiors, 2 Alba Place, Portobello Road, London. Visual by Caroline Aitken.

Right: 'Prints for the Collector, Designer and Decorator' by the O'Shea Gallery, 89 Lower Sloane Street, London.

Everything in the Garden is Lovely . . .

THIS YEAR'S British Interior Design Exhibition, to be held at the Chelsea Old Town Hall in London from 24 May until 17 June, will take the garden as a recurrent theme.

The event commences with a charity gala evening on 23 May in aid of the National Society for the Prevention of Cruelty to Children to be attended by Princess Margaret. The official opening on 24 May will be performed by Princess Alexandra. The 25-day event will act as a showcase for the talents of 28 eminent designers in a variety of individual room-sets. Whether design is to be employed in a home office, bedroom, cellar retreat or drawing room, there will be much to inspire. A rather unusual interpretation of this year's garden theme will appear in one of **Miriam Cobrin's Designs** to combine a dressing room with an internal garden in 'room for change'. Other sets with garden themes will be used by **The Chelsea Gardener** and **Carter Fulcher Tate** who are to decorate the raised stage area, and **Martin Robinson Flowers** to create a potting shed.

As a contrast, new work ethics and the use of computers at home provides **David Hicks International** with the inspiration for a 'study in white'. Here a home office will be designed to make best use of the serenity of the home and the advances of new technology in the workplace. A dramatic scheme for a drawing room in an international hotel is to be provided by **Broosk Interior Designs.** The **Harrods' Interior Design Studio,** whose new look is being created by Robin Mackay and Dallas Herbert, will be aiming to show the worth of interior architecture as opposed to 'mere cosmetic decoration'.

For the traditional period home, **Sudeley Castle Furniture** will be exhibiting a new range of hand-made furniture in a setting by theatre designer Max Stewart. Private retreats are the focus of **Jenny Armit Interiors** who is to incorporate a temperature-controlled wine cabinet into an elegant cellar-like room-set. The cooling effects of blue, cream and beige tones are to be put to good use in **Joanna Wood's** eighteenth-century-style bedroom set. While **Smallbone** is to launch a new kitchen, designed by Jonny Grey to make good use of natural materials and British craft skills in an 'unfitted' look.

For the best room-sets on display there are to be two new awards to be given by *House and Garden* magazine, and *The World of Interiors*. Bonham's auction house is to hold a special auction of furniture, architectural fittings, and furnishings at the exhibition on Thursday 14 June at 6.30 pm.

● The exhibition will be open to the public from 11 am on 24 May. Opening hours are as follows: Monday to Friday 10.30 to 6 pm, Wednesday 10.30 to 7 pm, Saturday and Sunday 11 pm to 5 pm. Admission for adults is £7 which includes a catalogue, and £4 for children under 14 years. There are reductions for students and special groups of 10 or more.

Above: 'Room for Change' an internal garden and dressing room by Miriam Cobrin Designs. Visual by Caroline Aitken.

Left: The 'Rotunda Bookroom' by Anthony Paine. Showing Greek doric and neo-classical influences.

AT HOME with Emma Bromidge

TONIGHT'S WEATHER: DRY — LATE PRICES EXTRA

Evening Standard

LONDON, WEDNESDAY, 23 MAY, 1990

All hands on

If you are creating a house to welcome London's top interior designers, who better to help you than . . . London's top interior designers?

CATHERINE STOTT visits a home where nothing has been left as it was

A LIFE IN THE HOME — Fleur Rosso...

WHEN Fleur Rosdale bought her Georgian house in Kensington's Pembroke Square she knew she would have to make extraordinary demands on its tall, narrow space.

'I planned the whole first-floor drawing-room around a big bargain'

INTERNATIONAL PRESS CUTTING BUREAU
Extract from: AIRPORT
-London-
MAY 1990

Best of British

Anyone with an interest in interior design should wend their way to Chelsea Old Town Hall in the King's Road between May 24 and June 17. **The British Interior Design Exhibition** was one of the great success stories of the late '80s, and offers a chance to see what's around amongst the trendy British designers.

Extract from: THIS IS LONDON
18 MAY 1990

WOMAN'S
JOURNAL
MAY 1990

DESIGN

Make a special date for the British Interior Design Exhibition; plus a look at the latest ranges in painted furniture, woodware, tiles . . . and chickens

DESIGN EXHIBITION OFFER

There is no excuse for missing this year's British Interior Design Exhibition—*Journal* readers who take along this page will be entitled to a discounted entrance fee of £5 (normally £7). This annual gathering of some of the best-known interior decorators in the business has become a firm date for all design enthusiasts. Twenty-eight exhibitors, each with their own room-set, will be taking part, including Derek Frost whose sketch for a study (above) gives a taste of what's in store. At Chelsea Old Town Hall, King's Road, London SW3 from 24th May to 17th June.

INTERNATIONAL PRESS
CUTTING BUREAU
Extract from: LONDON LOG
-London-
MAY 1990

■ One of the great success stories of the 1980s, **The British Interior Design Exhibition** is ready to lead the way into the 1990s. Now in its third year, it is firmly established as the premier showcase for interior design in Britain. The 28 participants in the 25 day event, represent a cross-section of interior design today. The event, which will be officially opened by Her Royal Highness Princess Alexandra at the Chelsea Old Town Hall on May 24, runs until June 17. Information: 071-938 4758/0.

LETTER FROM LONDON

LETTER FROM LONDON
14 HEALEY STREET
LONDON
NW1 8SR

MAY 24-JUN 17: THE BRITISH INTERIOR DESIGN EXHIBITION once again shows us the best with 28 top designers creating rooms. Good for contacts if you want to employ a designer and ideas if you want to do it yourself. The Gala Evening for the NSPCC is

what's on ● where to go ● what to do ● what's on ● where to go ● what to do ● what's on

Top flower show is set for record crowd

CHELSEA expects to attract a record 20... during the four day flower show at the Ro... grounds beginning on Tuesday.

They will include the Royal Family wi... visitors to the top floral event of the year in ... ticultural and social calendars which the Ro... tural Society began in 1914.

Admission costs for the two public day... Thursday (£7 after 4pm) and £12 for all da...

For the first time in its history the show... agency — Keith Prowse. Postal applicatio... made Chelsea Flower Show Ticket Office...

For credit card booking ring 071-748 14...

Chelsea look forward another big occasi... hold their British Interior Design Exhib... Chelsea Old Town Hall from Thursday ... June 17.

Also, The Green Consumer Exhibition, ... the New Life Designs, will be held at the Ro... tural Halls, Westminster, from Thursday ... Monday May 28. For details ring 071-938...

This runs together with the Festival fo... Spirit by the same organisers.

Other events being held in town this mon... Rainforest Festival organised by the Friend... at the Barbican Centre From May 27 unti... riders are looking forward to the Evening ... Displays at the Hyde Park Riding Arena on ... 29.

On May 31, The Fine Arts and Antiques ... the Olympia, West Kensington. This will r... 10 but will be closed on June 4.

INTERNATIONAL PRESS
CUTTING BUREAU
Extract from: BROMLEY ADVERTISER
-Kent-
MAY 1990

THE INDEPENDENT

TUESDAY 29 MAY 1990

SPECIAL OFFERS

See Matisse's Odalisque, Harmony in Red, 1926-27, among 20th-century masterpieces loaned from the private Gelman collection. The exhibition is at the Royal Academy of Arts (see list), which is offering *Independent* readers £1.10 off the full admission price of £3.50. Present this voucher at the ticket office. (Not valid for those on concessionary rates).

Interior Design
Independent readers are offered reduced admission to the British Interior Design Exhibition, a showcase for interior design, at Chelsea Old Town Hall until 17 June. Among the 28 designers giving a taste of their work through room-sets, and perhaps inspiring a little D-I-Y creativity in visitors, are Joanna Wood, who reproduces an 18th-century-style four-poster bed as the focal point of her bedroom, and Anthony Paine, who drew on Greek doric and neo-classical influences for a "Rotunda Bookroom".

Present this voucher at the door to pay £4 instead of £7 (includes catalogue). *King's Rd, London SW3 (071-938 4758). Mon-Fri 10.30am-6pm, Wed 10.30am-7pm, Sat-Sun 11-5pm.*

Symposium
"Art Creating Society", a three-day international symposium, exhibition and series of commissioned projects, will take place in Oxford from 1-3 June. It sets out to examine the meaning of art beyond the museum environment. An international group of artists, curators and art theorists will be debating issues like "Art Creating Society" and "Art as a Social Process".

It has been organised by the Museum of Modern Art in Oxford, which is offering *Independent* readers who book for three days, a £5 discount off the £15 cost. Book by phone and present coupon on arrival.
30 Pembroke St (0865-722733). Symposium, 1-3 June; exhibition, 1-10 June.

INTERNATIONAL PRESS-CUTTING BUREAU
224-236 Walworth Road,
London SE17 1JE
Extract from
The Times – London.

& BRIEFLY

Designs for living

INTERNATIONAL PRESS-CUTTING BUREAU
224-236 Walworth Road,
London SE17 1JE
Extract from
Time Out – London.
30 MAY 1990

SPECIAL EVENTS

Chelsea kaleidoscope

The British Interior Design Exhibition is well established as a forum for interior design ideas and is now setting the pace for the 1990s. Belinda Peel previews some of this year's rooms, illustrated here in artists' impressions

Interior design has become such a pervasive creative force that it now extends beyond the home to offices, hotels and, in a curious way, to gardens. This is the principle underlying the third staging of the British Interior Design Exhibition, at Chelsea Old Town Hall from May 24 to June 17.

Once again, the exhibition has attracted some of the best interior design talent around, firmly establishing itself as a premier event in the summer calendar. Twenty-eight designers are taking part this year, producing a cross-section of room-sets in a variety of styles, from traditional to avant-garde, as can be seen in our selection of drawings depicting the rooms.

Many of the designers at this year's exhibition have addressed the problem of incorporating high-tech appliances into traditional domestic interiors. As we become more reliant on computers and other machines, designers have had to ... ways to integrate these essential components. In partnership with Angus Gibson Music, Nicholas Hoslam shows in his 'Music Room' that audio, television and satellite equipment can be installed in a discreet and pleasing manner.

Another designer who has successfully tackled this problem is Stephen Ryan, chief designer of David Hicks International. His classically elegant 'Study in White' interprets the modern work ethic of computers and electronics in a domestic interior.

David Hicks, himself, has also contributed to the exhibition in a set which emphasises the importance of blending interior and exterior views. His disciplined approach to design is well suited to a formal courtyard, designed in conjunction with The Chelsea Gardener, which has also teamed up with George Carter of Carter Fulcher Tate on a theatrical garden scheme. The Chelsea Gardener has a total of four garden sets, all exploring the relationship between architecture, interior design and gardening, an idea taken further in Miriam Cobrin's unusual combination of ...

... the continuing influence of classical architecture on contemporary design. Similar influences can be discerned in the cool, elegant bedroom put together by Robin Mackay and Dallas Herbert of Harrods Interior Design Studio.

In contrast, Joanna Wood's bedroom is an essay in romanticism, using a stunning eighteenth-century-style four-poster bed as focal point, with sumptuous floral fabrics in yellow and blue for furnishings.

This polarity underlines one of the most significant aspects of the ...

INTERNATIONAL PRESS-CUTTING BUREAU
224-236 Walworth Road,
London SE17 1JE
Extract from
Sunday Telegraph – London.

Rooms for manoeuvre

The British Interior Design Exhibition shows the experts changing tack to keep up to date, reports Anoop Parikh

ONE OF the most reliable and glamorous guides to the decorating world made its reappearance this week. The British Interior Design Exhibition is back at Chelsea Old Town Hall in the King's Road for its annual three-week season. It shows that interior designers are in one of their regular periods of flux.

Architect Miriam Cobrin's 'Room for Change' is a dressing-room that looks out onto an internal garden. Gravel, water and silvery foliage complement the terracotta-orange and aqua-blue colour scheme. "I wanted a secret space," she says.

INTERNATIONAL PRESS CUTTING BUREAU
Extract from: MARIE CLAIRE
-London-
JUN 1990

INTERIORS
Design for Living

trend in interior design — Irish style
British Interior Design Exhibition

By Mary Cross

No gimmicks

Sophisticated

Kerry

Contracts

ARREDO
INCONTRI A TEMA
tessili complementi
n.3 international edition

HOUSTON
Lifestyle & Entertainment
Houston Chronicle
Section D
Saturday, June 9, 1990

Where's the chintz?

Don't expect English country look at designer showhouse in London

英国
EIKOKU
UK £1.30
JAPAN ¥500
THE JAPANESE MAGAZINE ON BRITAIN

3rd British Interior Design Exhibition
Chelsea Old Town Hall, King's Road, London SW3

CASA VOGUE, SPAIN JUNE '90

LONDRES

DISEÑO DE INTERIOR BRITANICO

INTERNATIONAL PRESS CUTTING BUREAU
Extract from: THE MAGAZINE
-London-
JUN 1990

Charlotte Bevan takes a trip around the world with three interior designers

WORLD Vision

The English country look, however jaded, is here to stay. We are, after all, a fiercely traditional, xenophobic lot. But there are certain designers who, dare one say it, an abhorrence of chintz who have combined their Englishness with foreign forms and in doing so have stretched their imaginations beyond frills, flowers and Folkstone.

MAY/JUNE 1990

HOME TEXTILES & FURNISHINGS Review

Leading the way into the 90's

DESIGN FOR A NEW DECADE

The San Diego Union
Homes

A new wave in BRITAIN

MINIMALIST FRILLS ARE THE LATEST LOOK IN INTERIOR DESIGN

CASA & JARDIM
MAIO 90

London

INTERNATIONAL PRESS CUTTING BUREAU
Extract from: ANTIQUES TRADE GAZETTE
-London-
JUN 1990

DAVID MOSS reports on fairs, markets and other Trade activities

Dealers' Dossier

Making contact with design world

The Directors of
The Interior Design House Limited
request the pleasure of your company at the
GALA PREVIEW
of
THE
BRITISH INTERIOR DESIGN
EXHIBITION
in the presence of
H.R.H. THE PRINCESS MARGARET
COUNTESS OF SNOWDON
in aid of
QUEEN ELIZABETH'S FOUNDATION
FOR DISABLED PEOPLE
at
1 Cambridge Gate
Regent's Park
London NW1 4JN
on Tuesday 3rd June 1997
R.S.V.P.
The Lord Kenilworth
and Joanna Wood
Q.E.F.D.
c/o Leatherhead Court
Leatherhead
Surrey KT22 0BN
Ticket Price
£55.00
Champagne
Reception
6.30pm to 9.00pm
ADMISSION BY TICKET ONLY

BIDE edition 9 (1997)

1 Cambridge Gate, Regent's Park, London

A selection of press cuttings from The British Interior Design Exhibition 1997 (BIDE). Exhibitors included: Sybyl Colefax & John Fowler, Woodstock Designs with Ian Walton Associates, Victoria Waymouth Interiors, Clifton Interiors, Lecchini Way Architects, Joanna Trading, Peter Wadley Architects, Atrium Limited, KLC School of Interior Design, Clarke & Thomas Interior Design, Ashton Products with Peter Wadley Architects, Charles CHesshire Landscape & Garden Design, Charles Rutherfoord with Brian Everest, G.A. Design International, Dargie Lewis Designs, Christophe Gollut, Baker Nevile Design Partnership, Jenny Armit Interiors, Omega Interiors, Stephen Ryan Design & Decoration, Alidad, Graça Viterbo, Tessa Kennedy Design, Charles Bateson at IDC, Jane Wolley Dod Garden Design with Lloyd Christie. Rolls-Royce ran a competition open to the BIDE exhibitors, which was won by Joanna Trading, the car was constructed at Crewe and was on show under an awning at the entrance throughout the run of the exhibition and was subsequently sold.

Design of the times

Do-it-yourself decorating is all ve[ry] well for the lucky few with an eye for what is intrinsically 'right'. Bu[t] …mph, there is … Belinda Buckl[ey] …litor of *Homes &* … explains why … er bringing in … turns the … of the leading … s interior desig[n]

BRITISH DESIGN

BRITISH INTERIOR DESIGN EXHIBITION 1997

In June 1997, The British Interior Design Exhibition, the UK's only designer-led interior design exhibition is being held (4th to 22nd June) at 1 Cambridge Gate, Regents Park, London. This unique show, open to the public and trade alike, will provide visitors with the opportunity to meet the designers, see the room exhibits and to source their own fabrics, paints, wallpaper etc. from the extensive exhibition catalogue. As a special feature of this event there will be the opportunity to attend special one-day interior design lecture courses to develop a deeper understanding of design concepts in the context of this exhibition.

1 Cambridge Gate is a magnificent 40-room Victorian town-house, set in the picturesque beauty of London's Regents Park. This huge house has provided 30 design teams, and over 350 supplier companies with the opportunity of transforming the interior of this totally restored building. The works of Jenny Armit, John Colefax & Sibyl Fowler, Tessa Kennedy, Victoria Weymouth, Joanna Wood, Christophe Gollut, Randle Siddeley, Stephen Ryan, Charles Rutherfoord, Christopher Nevile,

exhibition

final curtai[n]

…ers of the

The British have always been reluctant to hire interior decorators, but, with their help, you can have the house – or room – of your dreams, without straining cheque book or sanity. *Caroline Clifton-Mogg* explains how

COUNTRY LIFE

SEPTEMBER 26, 1996 EVERY THURSDAY £2

INTERIOR DECORATION

Plus … Blair's … values: exclusive … terview

THE BRIT[ISH] … DESIGN … Londres de 4 a…

THE WOR[LD OF] INTER[IORS]

AD

ARCHITECTURAL DIGEST. LE PIU BELLE CASE DEL MONDO

AMBIENTE

Ogni stanza uno stile

VARIE PROPOSTE D'ARREDO IN UNA DIMORA VITTORIANA

AMBIENTE

Ogni stanza uno stile

[L]UXURIATE AND LEARN

SPECIAL READER OFFER

INTERIORES

Con acento inglés

Un grandioso edificio victoriano fue el escenario de «The British Interior Desing Exhibition», la más importante muestra decorativa que se lleva a cabo en Londres desde hace siete años.

TEXTO: MARIYA MESEGUER

Con la participación de treinta decoradores reunidos en un espacio de unos 1.600 m², distribuidos en seis plantas y el sótano, la muestra The British Interior Design Exhibition, representativa del más típico estilo inglés, contó con pocas aportaciones nuevas, salvo excepciones como la de Charles Bateson, que proyectó un pequeño apartamento en el ático, al que consiguió dar un toque de carácter y elegancia mediante el novedoso tratamiento de las paredes, a base de pan de plata y oro, y el perfecto acabado de los muebles, de madera naturales. También destacó la portuguesa Graça Viterbo, que con telas de Braquenie definió el estilo fresco y delicado de un dormitorio con cuarto de baño integrado. Por su parte, Joana Trading y Joan Somerville, autores del salón de la planta baja, con paredes de grandes cuarterones de madera teñida en color natural y dos ambientes bien definidos, ofrecieron un perfecto ejemplo de cómo ambientar un espacio a base de butacas y butacones de distintos estilos, aligerando el tradicional espacio repleto de «sofás».

... con una gran cocina en la que destaca el movimiento del techo y una graciosa zona de paso de estética minimalista. 3. Italiano, elegante, recargado y masculino, cuarto de baño diseñado por Tessa Kennedy y Chris Watkins. 4. Joanna Wood y Joan Somerville demostraron cómo ambientar un espacio con butacas y sillones que aligeran un lugar tradicionalmente lleno de sofás. 5. Jane Wolley ideó esta terraza, pequeña pero cuidada, que se decoró con un cenador y mobiliario de madera de teca. 6. Para decorar las paredes del ático, Charles Bateson utilizó láminas de pan de oro y de plata.

Una mezcla perfecta. A pesar de que esta casa está reformada por varios decoradores y diseñadores, el resultado es sorprendentemente homogéneo. En el centro, mesa de café, de la anticuaria Mary Fox Linton, y al fondo, otra de marquetería, de David Linley. Toda la iluminación corrió a cargo de The Study, con la colaboración de John Cullen Lighting.

Luz en el suelo. Un detalle del foco incrustado en el suelo (véase Notas Plus), resalta la textura de las cortinas de Sacho Hesslein. Tratándose de un país de cielo gris, este tipo de iluminación, combinada con unas cortinas transparentes, da excelentes resultados ambientales.

Baldosas hidráulicas. La entrada de la casa es, quizá, la zona menos afectada por la reforma. Llama la atención el suelo, de baldosas hidráulicas (véase Notas Plus), y las paredes, con un zócalo de madera azul, y el resto, en un atrevido naranja. Los apliques son un diseño de Mark Brazier Jones.

INTERIOR
ITION
nho de 1997

Design solutions

Alidad

The phrase 'bedsit' conjures up many images, but it is unlikely that any of them coincide with Alidad's idea of such a room, in this case on the third floor of the house. 'I thought of this as the main guest bedroom,' he explains. 'As the room was big enough to have both a bed and a proper seating-area, I decided to make it almost a grand bedsit, as if it were the converted top floor of a *palazzo*, with all the temporal and spiritual comforts that a well-travelled man of the world might need.' Those comforts include not only books and music but also an advanced computer system relaying vital information, including the latest share prices, from behind a set of doors in the dressing-area, a design principle Alidad describes as 'traditional on the outside and high-tech behind the scenes'.

The ceilings in this part of the house were not high enough for Alidad. His solution was simplicity itself: he just ignored the problem. Against stamped-leather walls he put in the largest possible pieces of furniture, working on the theory that small pieces of furniture emphasize the scale of a small space, whereas large objects make the same space seem larger. The dressing-room is decorated with an elaborate *trompe-l'œil* imitating inlaid wood; the walls of the adjoining bathroom have a dry plaster finish. With three nuances of a single mood, this is the bedsit of a latter-day Grand Tourist □

Alidad's 'grand bedsit' contains a club fender from Acres Farm, a sofa from Howard Chairs and Grand Tour souvenirs from Christopher Hodsoll.

Readers' event

Readers of *House & Garden* are invited to a private view at the British Interior Design Exhibition on June 9, from 6.30–8.30pm. This will be a splendid opportunity to meet all the participating designers, as well as organizer Fleur Rossdale, in relaxed and convivial circumstances. For information on how to obtain tickets, please see page 86. For the BIDE ticket hotline, call 0181-944 2344.

Design solutions

'Styles at the exhibition range from the purely traditional to bare Minimalism'

Peter Wadley

What do you do when asked to transform changing-rooms, a couple of passages and a staircase or two? Not a very inspiring project, you might think. Perhaps you could paint it magnolia and shut the door? Or – if you were Peter Wadley – you could formulate a conceit involving visual puns and imaginative design. 'The main practical problem was the headroom, or lack of it: the ceilings were very low. I felt the whole area needed to be more like an artistic installation than a conventional plan.'

One spiral staircase led up to the swimming-pool, another descended to the kitchen. To unify these various elements and increase circulation space, Peter redesigned the whole area, eliminating most of its angles and replacing them with curves, in the form of gentle waves of wall sloping around the space. The wall in front of the steam-room is painted with a large mural by Martin Fuller, one of several artists commissioned to make artwork for the area. In other places, Peter Wadley has set mirrored walls at right angles to each other to quadruple the perceived space. White stone floors complement blue and white Portland stone stair-treads and tiled staircase walls, their tones intended to imitate descending strata of the earth's crust. Lighting is with fibre-optics: points of light wash over everything. It is, Peter says, 'a visual treasure hunt.' ▷84

Peter Wadley's imaginative unification of previously disparate spaces contains, among other works, a carved wooden falcon by Julian Stanley and the Oscar Chair by Ashton Products.

Design solutions

Colefax and Fowler

Vivien Greenock of Colefax and Fowler was assigned the first-floor dining-room, a testing commission because, in her opinion, the traditional dining-room is increasingly an anachronism: 'A dining-room to me conjures up thoughts of cooks, butlers and maids – and I wanted to design an inviting room, where people could sit and eat and live,' she explains.

The room itself was huge, dark and uninteresting, so instead of a long, central table, she divided the room into distinct areas, with a round table in the middle and another in the window as a breakfast or work table, which could also be combined with the central table for large dinners. She also opted to include two separate, upholstered seating-areas on opposite sides of the room. These give the room a softer look and make it more inviting. The walls are padded and covered with material, which has two benefits: the acoustics are better and the atmosphere is cosier. The colours are bright and sunny. Squares of matting on the floor strike a note of informality in this latter-day evocation of a traditional, English country-house 'Eating Room'.

Vivien Greenock's design for the first-floor dining-room features Colefax and Fowler's 'Oakley' chintz.

Joanna Wood

The vast sitting-room on the ground-floor (seventy-four square metres) turned out to be the ultimate challenge for Joanna Wood. 'Its shape was very difficult to deal with. Although it is so large, it has doors at both ends; this meant it could have ended up looking like a huge corridor,' Joanna remembers. 'Then there was the oak linenfold panelling – circa 1925, dark, dreary, very *Hammer House of Horror* and listed; and all I can say about the chimneypiece is that it is absolutely hideous.'

The oak panelling was bleached 'all the way back', then waxed to bring out the soft, grey tones of the wood. A very large Ben Nicholson painting obscures the upper part of the chimneypiece. Either side of the fire-place are large cabinets, designed to house sitting-room essentials – drinks, sound-system and television.

The unusually large floor area necessitated more than one focal point: 'I felt the traditional central focus wouldn't work, so instead we arranged the seating at either end of the room and placed in the centre two large, French provincial chairs.' The heavy, coffered ceiling was painted with a *trompe-l'œil* design which continues to the top of the panelling, thereby pulling together all the diverse parts of this once heavy room. ▷73

'Canevas de Tourain' fabric from Claremont and a Vaughan urn in the sitting-room.

Design solutions

'Designers' work can be seen at its most inventive and imaginative'

British Interior Design Exhibition 1997

Can British design be exported?

exhibition

Can British interior design be categorized, or can it be described as eclectic? How do British interior designers conduct themselves with reference to the export market? A focus on the British Interior Design Exhibition (BIDE) 1997 reveals vastly contrasting views and approaches.

The exhibition was unveiled in a magnificent five-floor Regents Park house in early June, to run for three weeks, and eclectic was the most bandied about word on the opening day.

A good example of eclecticism would be Jenny Armit Interiors' morning room and Omega Interiors' bedroom suite, just across the corridor from each other, but two totally different planets...

Armit's pale sycamore floor was designed to give a deceptive wave effect, as you enter the room you can almost see it undulating. Her chairs were protected by dainty "frocks" - "I was tempted to add high heeled shoes," said Armit. Her sofas were curved, feline and bright, bright yellow, black and white photos were dwarfed by massive white frames and painted black stones evoking a typical English beach in shape were arranged neatly round a miniature landscape garden. Charming with a touch of wacky sophistication, a place to sip elderflower cordial and paint on multicoloured nail varnish.

Omega's bedroom suite was created for an imaginary client, an aesthete who "was gorgeous in his twenties but went a bit seedy," according to designer Philip Hopper. Luxury, masculinity, a swathed four poster, a tiny television in the bathroom to alleviate the boredom of shaving, a pile of Conran Shop soaps priced about HK$100 each and a display of austerely matching writing implements.

This is one small example of the contrast offered at the BIDE. Whether British interior designers are eclectic or not is a crucial point of debate when the issue of exporting is raised.

"There is a big demand for British designers abroad because of their

'Witness the launch of many exciting new products, from furniture to fittings.'

Left page:
Living space by Charles Bateson, 1 Cambridge Gate,
Regent's Park, BIDE 1997

This page:
First floor drawing room by Christophe Gollut, 1
Cambridge Gate, Regent's Park, BIDE 1997
Gentleman's retreat by Alidad, 1 Cambridge Gate,
Regent's Park, BIDE 1997

50 BRUXELLES — Gare Maritime

Hôtel de la Poste: an attractive and inclusive multipurpose environment hosting IIDE 2018 and 2019

Situated on the Brussels Canal, Hôtel de la Poste started life in the 19th Century as an office building within the former train station and industrial site of Tour & Taxis. The administrative heart of the complex, Hôtel de la Poste was long disused having lost importance as a shipping and customs hub.

It is Tour & Taxis' vision to create an attractive and inclusive multipurpose environment that offers the optimal balance of diverse accommodation, next-generation workspaces, and state-of-the-art event venues. Hôtel de la Poste will embody this vision as a place where people come to connect, feel inspired, and grow together as professionals and invididuals.

Continuing to host cultural events in the main hall at Hôtel de la Poste, the upper floors of this magnificent venue have recently been restored, ten rooms decorated by international designers for Salon IIDE.
These "Salons", which used to belong to the railway station, have been unseen for 40 years.

The redevelopment process of Tour & Taxis has prioritised giving a modern interpretation to the historic buildings on the site, while respecting their authenticity and architectural heritage.
Hôtel de la Poste is the latest example of this focus: the original character of the building has been preserved, respected, and celebrated in its redevelopment.

Next double page: detail of a porcelain light sculpture by Coup-de-foudre.

Foyer

The International Interior Design Exhibition
Brussels

EDITION 10

Photography: Miguel Etchepare

Hôtel de la Poste
Tour & Taxis
7 rue Picard, B-1000 Brussels
www.iide.be

List of exhibitors

1	Michel Penneman	*Belgium*
2	Christophe Remy	*Belgium*
3	J.PHINE	*Netherlands*
4	Erik Dhont	*Belgium*
5	Christophe Gollut	*UK*
6	Gert Voorjans	*Belgium*
7	Carter Tyberghein	*UK*
8	Jessie Lecomte	*Belgium*
9	Henrietta Spencer-Churchill	*UK/USA*
10	Olivier Lapidus	*France*

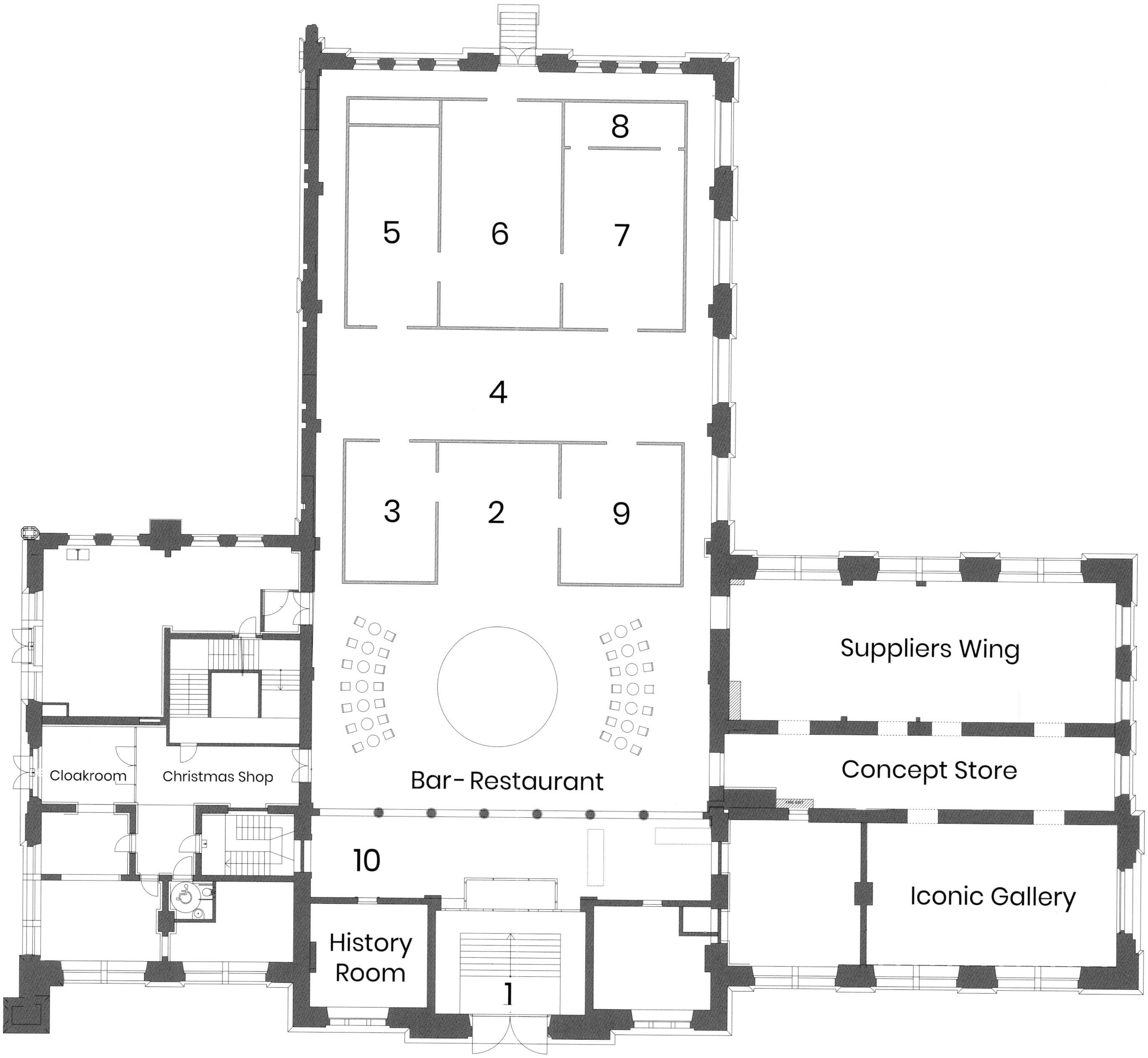

Next double page :

1 & 2. Living space by Gert Voorjans
3 & 5. Restaurant in the main hall at Hotel de la Poste, 5 rue Picard.
4 & 9. Lamps by Rene Houben, rugs by Ashtari carpets, floor by Rudy de Keyser, speakers by Alpha high end.
6. Arthus Gallery with Anita Le Grelle, Light it up & Arnold de Vinck.
7. Interior detail by Patrick Tyberghein.
8. Assistant Anna Berntson with Caro Rossdale helping out.

Room 1

Forest of Light
Michel Penneman

 Photography: Andreas von Einsiedel

Michel Penneman: balance of beauty and function

Michel Penneman heads a multi-cultural team creating interiors for the home, offices, restaurants and hotels. Working internationally, the practice prides itself with their attention to detail, ambiance, lighting and comfort to ensure that their client is at home and at ease with the environment created for each project they undertake.

First and foremost, they specialize in concepts.
Michel's designs for the Perfumery "l'Antichambre", the Watch shop "Hall of Time", the "Pierre Marcolini" Stores in Taiwan and Monaco, the "Yadoya" & the "Hygge" Hotels, the "Rob Restaurant" met with enthusiastic response. Designing a hotel is a white page for Penneman, where he tells a story.

As well as the multi-award-winning Pantone Hotel, various other hotels designed by Michel have also been recognised.
Tenbosch House won first prize in the B&B Hotel category of Commerce Design Brussels, as did the "Zoom Hotel" and the "Hygge Hotel".
Each project covers both the aesthetic and technical feats, Michel Penneman focuses on acoustics, lighting, tone, texture and colour. Projects are always customized and ingenious, providing a high level of comfort, whilst creating the desired image.

For almost 20 years, Michel Penneman has pushed boundaries in design concepts.
For him, a space tells a story about the people that occupy it. As an interior architect, Penneman works first with the space, addressing each issue to ensure bespoke individuality. From this viewpoint he creates boutiques, homes and commercial space. Nothing is left to chance, always keeping a balance between functionality and beauty.

Penneman likes the challenge of creating uplifting space for private clients, reflecting their personality and interests.

Michel Penneman, Interior Designer
3 avenue Macau, B-1050 Brussels
T +32 (0)2 649 19 11
M. +32 (0)475 71 76 79
www.michelpenneman.com
mp@michelpenneman.com

Room 2

The Silent Pool Gin Bar by
Christophe Remy

 Photography: Miguel Etchepare

Christophe Remy: designs with timeless charm

Behind curtains, Christophe Remy works on all fronts. His mission? Imagine interiors and showcase shops, boost up the fame of a name, identification with a universe as much as maximizing the power of the image, of a logo and of storytelling.

With its old Europe style, this artistic director / art adviser / decorator picks up the fashion sphere. In a world where trends pass, his creations retain a timeless charm weathered by the patina of time. Between private residences and trendy boutiques, he knows how to impose his style until making everything he touches ultra-desirable.

As an admirer of the decorators-designers of the past, Christophe Remy undertakes a contemporary rereading of his influences.
He loves sharp architectures, stretched lines, graphic ornaments...
His interiors come from bold mixtures of materials, contrasts, without a priori. The writing of his work tends towards a subtle association of refinement, comfort and radicality. A simple, readable decoration and architecture.

A taste for the metamorphosis of the classic. No false décor: he likes to work with noble materials and his choices are clearly stated. He often mixes genres and does not remain frozen in one universe.

Christophe Remy
M. +32 (0) 476 68 66 62
www.christopheremy.net
chris@christopheremy.net

Room 3

The living space

J.PHINE

 Photography: Andreas von Einsiedel

Nannette and Natasja (J. PHINE) with artist Kaye McGarva in their IIDE room.

J.PHINE: a total concept for your home

With distinguished careers that include working for the globally renowned designer Piet Boon, Nannette and Natasja are very happy to have joined forces in a new venture with the launch J.PHINE – a conceptual studio that aims to inspire clients into a completely new way of thinking about the interior in which they wish to live, work or enjoy.

How the J.PHINE Studio works:
We meet to discuss your lifestyle, individual style, design wishes and inspirations.
We design a total concept for your home as per the brief, share our aesthetic vision, produce a layout, introducing colour, materials and lighting for both the interior and exterior.
We develop the 'look and feel' into detailed drawings, offering a choice of colours and materials for each individual space; from the entrance to the master bedroom.
We handpick a team of trusted technical drafts-persons, furniture makers, artisans, contractors and suppliers per project, keeping technical details and functionality in mind.
We complement the design by fine-tuning the furniture, objets d'art and styling.

In other words: the signature style of your new home. Concept design / initial layouts / 2D+3D drawings / lighting plan /millwork / furniture plan / styling

For the living room in IIDE 2018, J.PHINE have collaborated with the artist Kaye McGarva (p. 64-65), Atelier Luxus (p. 66-67), Hanneke Beaumont (sculpture on page 58), Orac Decor, Van Boven Architecten, Schoenmakers Natuursteen and Spazio Nobile.

On pages 56-57 a number of recent residential projects by J. PHINE in the Netherlands.

J.PHINE
Maximiliaanstraat 17B, NL- Rotterdam
M.+31 (0) 6 38543006
www.jphine.com
nannette@jphine.com

J.PHINE
Zwaerdencroonstraat 24, NL- Rotterdam
M. +31 (0) 6 2840773
www.jphine.com
natasja@jphine.com

 Photography: Andreas von Einsiedel

TRACES by Kaye McGarva

Words by Meagan Seawright

Long gliding on
White light reflections.
I turn my eye to
See
Really
See
It's a given that I will crumple this vantage
From within
My own bias.
Momentarily,
I court perspective.
Finding infinity in paint.
No longer contained,
All waves disperse.
I am
Energy.

Artist Kaye McGarva describes her approach to abstract painting as playing with shadows. Her intriguing trompe l'oeil style creates a sense of uncertainty designed to challenge our perceptions.

Based in New Zealand, Kaye McGarva was hand picked to create an artwork in collaboration with young Dutch design company, J.Phine for IIDE 2018. Despite the geographic distance between them the shared minimalist aesthetic made for an easy and enjoyable collaboration. Kaye's work, Traces, a white on white abstract painting became the centerpiece for the room. Integral to the success of the design was using art as the starting point.

Kaye McGarva's work can be viewed at Macadam Gallery in Brussels and Muse gallery in New Zealand.

Contact details for Kaye McGarva:
macadamgallery.com
www.museart.nz
www.k-mcgarva.nz
T: +64 272899103
E: kayemcgarva@gmail.com
IG: kayemcgarvaartist

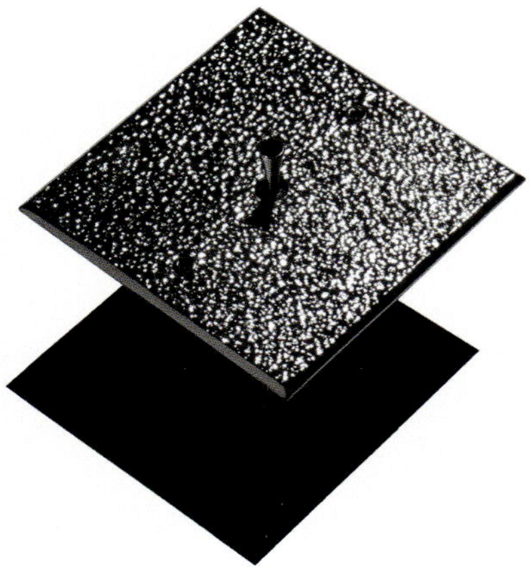

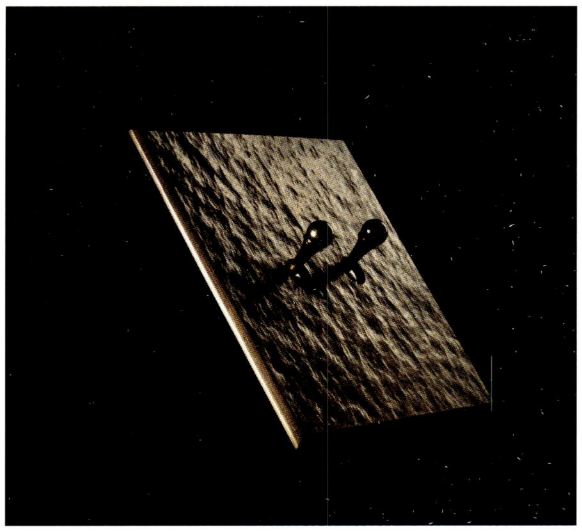

 Photography: Aurélien Lacroix

Atelier Luxus: handmade switches

Atelier Luxus creates meticulously handmade switches using materials of unparalleled quality and precision-tailored technology.

Developed over 20 years, Atelier Luxus combines brass with ultra-flat socket plates in multiple finishes.

Quality and attention to detail guide each step to meet technical and aesthetic challenges: refined design, precision manufacturing, craftsmanship, authenticity and luxury.

atelier luxus
Rue de la Baronnerie 9, B-4920 HARZE
www.atelierluxus.com
www.luxonov.com
info@atelierluxus.com
T: +32 (0)4 344 44 51

Room 4

Courtyard garden
by Erik Dhont

 Photography: Andreas von Einsiedel

Erik Dhont: Garden Design as a form of art

Erik Dhont sees Garden Design as a form of art, and he embraces it with imagination in order to give his clients a place to dream. Gardens are not only places to enjoy and appreciate life, but also places to grow and heal.

No matter if the commission is to restore an old garden or to realize a new one: the design emphasis is always on the process of discovering and conceptualizing elements from the past with the practical demands imposed by the present.
Functionality is balanced with a fine aesthetic that remains sensitive to the needs of the daily use, the environmental issues, and the surrounding landscapes.

Over the years Erik Dhont has developed a style that remains personal, distinctive and instantly recognizable. Organic shapes on paper are translated into real sculptural forms which gain their patina as time goes by and the garden matures. It is this changing sense of rhythm that flows between days, seasons and periods of life that Dhont aims to highlight in his design. And his gardens are spaces where this rhythm is embodied and performed.

The inner courtyard of the International Interior Design Exhibition 2018 has been enhanced by the presence of a temporary installation designed as the ultimate abstraction of an autumnal Garden.
A luxury harvest of hazel branches, rose hips and climbers have guided the visitors through the space, while the elegant geometries of wooden pedestals offered the sight of precious artefacts: vases, models and plaster works. This hybrid collection of many different elements made for an overwhelming experience, and transformed the visit in a journey of discovery between Nature and Life.

Erik Dhont
Rue du Marché au Porcs 30, B-1000 Brussels
T +32 2 219 19 02
www.erikdhont.com

Room 5

The collectors study
Christophe Gollut

 Photography: Andreas von Einsiedel

Christophe Gollut: an innate sense of style

Christophe Gollut came to London to study Interior Design at the Inchbald School of Design after reading law in his native Switzerland.
He has since become one of the leading decorators in London.

Christophe's talent, together with his attention to detail and innate sense of style has an element of 'Englishness' with a European twist. Entering a room designed by Christophe Gollut is always a pleasure. The atmospheres he creates overwhelm the senses with colour, texture and mystery. Each space is tailored to the individual in the context of the architecture of the building, its setting and prevailing climate.

Christophe is not formulaic in his approach and works with an educated instinct, an intuition for understanding the most appropriate treatment for the space in hand. He can be simple or elaborate, always giving the same meticulous attention to detail while achieving the impression that his rooms have been created through casual evolution.

Christophe has undertaken numerous projects, including offices and embassies, but now mostly concentrates on residential contracts all over the world.

Christophe Gollut
2 Collingham Place, Flat 3, London SW5 0PY
Tel. +44(0) 207 370 4123
www.christophegollut.com
gollut@christophegollut.com

Room 6

The salon
by Gert Voorjans

 Photography: Andreas von Einsiedel

Gert Voorjans: magical roomscapes

Gert Voorjans' exhilarating environments reflect the singular audacity of his vision. His unexpected juxtapositions of beautiful, surprising, provoking, and unique objects, works of art, and sculptural furniture elements constantly challenge the way we think about how we live today.

There is no place for timid, mundane, or formulaic in his design vocabulary, instead Gert's brilliantly coloured world celebrates the daring and the exceptional. His magical roomscapes ignite our imaginations, fuel our dreams, and enhance our realities.

These are exciting rooms for thoughtful people.

For his Salon at IIDE 2018, Gert collaborated with Van Den Weghe (marble), Tekna lighting, Rudy De Keyzer (bespoke wooden flooring), Alpha High End Music Systems, Spazio Nobile, Dankers Artisan Painters, Ashtari carpets and René Houben.

Gert Voorjans, Architectual and Design Practice
Leopoldplaats 11, B-2000 Antwerp
Tel. +32 (0)3 233 87 15
www.gertvoorjans.com
studio@gertvoorjans.com

Room 7

Bedroom and sitting room
by Carter Tyberghein

Carter Tyberghein: innovative solutions

Over the last two decades, award-winning designers Carter Tyberghein, have acquired a reputation for unique and elegant interiors ranging across the breadth of private residential homes, luxury residential developments to boutique hotels. Timeless, eclecticism and clarity are their motto to create inspired designs.

Patrick Tyberghein leads the London based design studio. Each commission is approached with a fresh and creative eye with the foresight to incorporate innovative solutions into each concept.

"A talented architectural team capable of large-scale vision executed with a light touch. Faultless space planning, purity of lines and boldness of scale are trademarks" (House & Garden Magazine).

Carter Tyberghein
1 Melbray Mews, Hurlingham Road, London SW6 3NS, United Kingdom
Tel. +44 20 7731 6557
www.cartertyberghein.com
patrick@cartertyberghein.com

Room 8

Interior lifestyle for dressing
by Jessie Lecomte

Jessie Lecomte: a room of intimacy

After graduating from the Antwerp Academy in 1996, Jessie Lecomte honed her skills, working with Belgium's top fashion houses before starting her own label in 2007.

In collaboration with IIDe, 'Grace of a Birds Wing', the name of her collection, was formulated as a feminine dressing room with attitude.

Carefully curated to emphasise the crossover between fashion and interior design, the room reflects colour and content; a room of intimacy. Jessie's designs frame a woman's body with the artful subtly of a Japanese Kimono, the feminine silhouette accentuated by her tailored sophisticated geometry. The pure forms of her clothes are enhanced by fastidious stitching, giving shape and movement. Pleats, tucks and twists emphasise the sharp and the edgy, producing tension and the unexpected.
Taking inspiration from contemporary art, ethnographic photography and pop culture, Jessie's vision is marked by stylish originality. Selecting textiles from the finest spun cashmere to stiff Japanese silks, often with layers of embroidery, print or beadwork, gives her collection an extraordinary quality. The interior, set in the context of fashion as art within an interior space, leads the visitor to understand the luxury of spending time in a designated room in which to select the perfect outfit to meet with the occasion.

Jessie Lecomte
Chemin des Oiseleurs 84, B-1180 Uccle,
M. +32 497 10 65 50
Tel. +32 2 347 19 94
www.jessielecomte.com
Insta. jessie_lecomte
info@jessielecomte.com

Photography: Andreas von Einsiedel

Room 9

The Breakfast room
Spencer-Churchill Designs

 Photography: Andreas von Einsiedel

Spencer-Churchill Designs: worldwide commissions

Henrietta Spencer-Churchill is the eldest daughter of The Late 11th Duke of Marlborough whose family home is Blenheim Palace in Oxfordshire.

Henrietta studied at the Inchbald School of Design before forming her own highly successful Interior Design Company, Woodstock Designs in 1981 undertaking commissions worldwide. Woodstock Designs are specialists in residential design from renovation of period properties to new build houses and experts in incorporating current trends and technology whilst respecting the historic character and architecture.

In 1986, Henrietta formed a separate Company, Spencer-Churchill Designs producing a selection of furniture, fabrics and wallpapers and since then her international success has enabled her to establish a US design company, Spencer-Churchill Designs Inc, in 2003.

Henrietta wrote her first book "Classic English Interiors" in 1990, followed by nine further books. Her eleventh, 'The Life of the House. The Evolution of Rooms' was published by Rizzoli in October 2012.

"I like to retain the style, interior architecture and character of each house, bringing services into the 21st century."

Spencer-Churchill Designs Ltd
7 High Street, Woodstock, Oxon, OX20 1TE (UK)
T. +44 (0) 1993 811887
www.spencerchurchilldesigns.com
oxford@woodstockdesigns.com

 Photography: Andreas von Einsiedel

Room 10

The Loggia Salon
by Olivier Lapidus

Olivier Lapidus: dialogue between luxury and innovation

In 1989, after spending many years in Japan, Olivier Lapidus, a graduate from the Ecole de la Chambre Syndicale de la Couture Parisienne who started his career at Pierre Balmain, took over his fathers' fashion house, Ted Lapidus, founded in Paris in 1951, as chief designer, which he ran until 2000. Olivier was awarded the prestigious distinction of the Dé d'Or de la Haute Couture in 1994.

Olivier's creativity revolves around a dialogue between luxury and innovation. He is the first couturier to engage with new technologies and the only one, to this day, who has harnessed them to direct his work. For years, his research has focused on integrating electronic elements into clothing, such as microencapsulated textiles, solar energy, fractal lace, as well as developing new plant-based fabrics and new printing techniques.

Cédric Brochier and Lapidus developed a technique introducing optical fibre into fabric at the Brochier's silk factory in Lyon. This major innovation, which brought together highly developed technology with traditional techniques, started a revolution in the world of decorative lighting, particularly in the medical field (luminotherapy), but also in other sectors such as aerospace and the automotive industry.

At IIDE, Olivier has brought together art, texture, light and colour to demonstrate his vision for an interior space, working with Dacryl and Ecart International. Ecart have included Olivier's own furniture designs and other collectors pieces. Olivier commissioned a large artwork by Krista Kim to complete his composition.

Known for the avant-garde, Olivier Lapidus' work continues to evolve, his legacy recognised as a major contribution to design.

https://creationolivierlapidus.paris

The International Interior Design Exhibition *Brussels*

EDITION 11

Previous left page :
Arte International wallpaper in this project
by Benedetti Interieur.

Hôtel de la Poste
Tour & Taxis
7 rue Picard, B-1000 Brussels
www.iide.be

List of exhibitors

FIRST FLOOR

Reception	*Welcome desk*
Collectors Gallery	*Vanessa Bruffaerts witth Pol Quadens*
Salon 1	*Diego Fortunato with Dedar*
Salon 2	*Fleur Rossdale for the interior design house*
Salon 3	*A.DEM Interiors with designers guild*
Bookshop	*Beta-Plus Publishing with Dominique Rigo*
Salon 4	*Gerald Watelet*

SECOND FLOOR

Salon 5 & 6	*Guimar Urbina interiors*
TheGallery	*Works by Johan Van Mullem*
Salon 7	*Benedetti interieur with Evolution21*
Salon 8	*LDécoration internationale*
Salon 9	*Maria Westerberg with Johan Patricny*
Bar/Restaurant	*Le Pain Quotidien*
The Terrace	*Isabelle Thiltgès sculpteur & Evolution21*
Salon 10	*Benedetti interieur with Casamance*

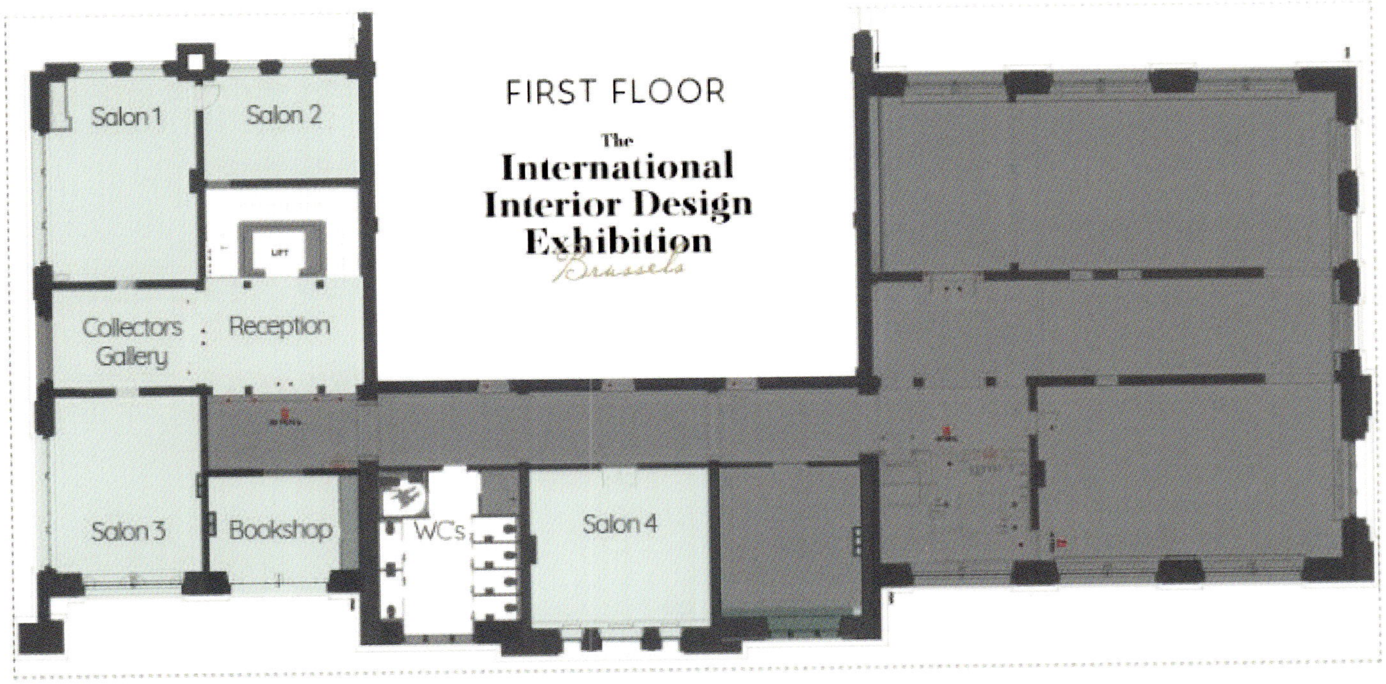
FIRST FLOOR
The
International
Interior Design
Exhibition
Brussels
Salon 1
Salon 2
LIFT
Collectors
Gallery
Reception
Salon 3
Bookshop
WC's
Salon 4

SECOND FLOOR
The
International
Interior Design
Exhibition
Brussels
LIFT
EXTERIOR
Terrace
Salon 10
EXTERIOR
Terrace
Bar
Restaurant
The Gallery
Salon 5
Salon 6
WC's
Salon 7
Salon 8
Salon 9

1. Sculpture by Diego Fortunato.
2. Artist Johan Van Mullem.
3. Gala evening.
4. & 5. Salon 10 by Benedetti Interieur.
6. 10. & 11. Sculptures by Isabelle Thiltgès
7. Recycled furniture by Maria Westerberg and her portrait by Johan Patricny.
11. Moooi wallpaper in the Benedetti Salon.
12. The cocktail bar at IIDE 2019 was managed by Julien de Meulemeester and Simon Chérot (start up company Frequency event partner).

Photography 1 and 8 : Vincent de Maeyer.

Salon 1

Diego Fortunato with Dedar

Photography:
Andreas von Einsiedel

Diego Fortunato with Dedar

Diego Fortunato is an artist and designer known for his ability to alter our perception and pleasure of both space and reality.

He founded his first design studio in 1995 in Barcelona, his London design studio followed in 2011. The Argentinian-born designer's lighting, urban furniture, rugs, upholstering, and limited edition objects reside between industrial design, sculpture and conceptual art.
Deceptively simple, yet meticulously detailed, they show his constant search for theoretically possible concepts rather than merely shapes.
He wants us to feel a story behind his work and sometimes his sense of humour and fantasy.
An accomplished designer, Diego has created long-lasting products for the market.
His timeless designs have become best-sellers over the years.

At IIDE, he has created Salon 1, adjacing the Collectors Gallery and the office / living room by Fleur Rossdale in collaboration with Dedar from Alinee, Galerie des Minimes, The Interior Design House, John Cullen Lighting, Vibia, Shade, Orac Decor, Van Den Weghe and Art Sablon Gallery.

Diego Fortunato
www.diegofortunato.com
diego@diegofortunato.com

Salon 2

Fleur Rossdale for The Interior Design House Ltd.

Photography:
Andreas von Einsiedel

Fleur Rossdale

Fleur Rossdale: impeccable sourcing

With a background in fine art, Fleur has run her design practice for over 15 years incorporating artworks into her interior schemes, often as turn key installations.
With a design ethic that adapts to place and context, Fleur works according to the brief, be it Classic or Contemporary.
Known personally to some of the most talented craftsmen in the world, Fleur's sourcing is impeccable.

For Salon 2 at IIDE, Fleur has collaborated with Pol Quadens, Marie's Corner, John Cullen Lighting, Vaughan Designs, Shade, Masureel, Emma Kennaway, Veedon Fleece, Orac Decor, Dacryl, Houlès, Evolution21, Benedetti Interieur and Tapissiers.

Fleur Rossdale
for The Interior Design House Ltd.
T +44 (07 887 681 311
fleur@fleurrossdale.com

Masureel: high-quality wallcoverings

Masureel is a 100% Belgian company that manufactures high-quality wallcoverings. Rooted in the heart of Flanders fields, the history of the company dates back to the 16th century. The Masureel family began with retting flax and gradually became an important leader in the textile industry. Art, craftsmanship and respect for nature characterize our brands (Khrôma, Zoom and Guy Masureel).

Guy Verstraete, the driving force of the company, has been a collector of modern and contemporary art for many years. These artworks form, in addition to a rich archive of wallpapers and textile samples, the beating heart of the company. The earliest works in the collection bear witness to the abstract movement of the 1920s. Parallel with the rise of modern industry, artists like Sonia Delaunay, Victor Servranckx, István (Etienne) Beöthy and others developed a new visual language that was based on pure principles of color and form. Many artists indulged in the field of the applied arts, in order to concretize their ideas and give shape to a new society. Within the same spirit, Masureel has always been driven to establish a synergy between art and industry, continuously innovating our creations in relation to technology.

Since art takes such a central role in our activity, we decided to develop a platform for research and production: MAF – Masureel Art Factory. Through artistic collaborations, we open up towards a more versatile comprehension of wallcovering design.

Being committed to the environment is for Masureel more than just a statement. We strive for minimal impact in our production facilities as well as for the materials we produce. While a fully degradable wallcovering is still behind the horizon, we are taking a step by step approach towards green innovation.

Masureel Internationaal
Kantstraat 1, B-8531 Hulste (Harelbeke)
www.masureel.com
info@masureel.com

Photography:
Alexandre Van Battel

Salon 3

A.DEM interiors with Designers Guild

Photography:
Andreas von Einsiedel

A.DEM interiors: eclectic and unique atmospheres

With more than 30 years of experience as an interior designer, Gilles de Meulemeester has just opened a new space, A.DEM interiors.

He presents his passions and his vocation to integrate his expertise in the transformation of residential and professional spaces with the creation of eclectic and unique atmospheres.

A.DEM interiors
Architecture d'intérieur - Décoration - Expositions - Mobilier
Rue Vanderkindere 277, B-1180 Uccle
T +32 (0)474 85 38 34
www.ademinteriors.be
contact@ademinteriors.be

Photography:
Andreas von Einsiedel

Designers Guild: inspirational home décor collections

Established in 1970 by Tricia Guild, Designers Guild designs and wholesales furnishing fabrics, wallcoverings, upholstery and bed and bath collections worldwide.

The Designers Guild Group employs over 280 people in the UK and overseas offices in Munich and Paris. 250 are in the UK, with a store and showrooms in Kings Road and Marylebone High Street, London, a 80,000 sq ft distribution centre and 16,000 sq ft purpose built head office, both in West London.
Rapid deliveries are guaranteed through a network of couriers and orders can be despatched anywhere in the UK, Europe and worldwide within 24 hours.

At IIDE 2019, Designers Guild wallpaper and fabrics were shown in Salon 3 by Gilles de Meulemeester (A.DEM interiors).

Designers Guild
Head Office
3 Latimer Place
London W10 6QT
T +44 (0)20 7893 7400
www.designersguild.com
info@designersguild.com

 Photography:
Andreas von Einsiedel

Salon 4

Gerald Watelet

Gerald Watelet: Haute Couture in interior design

Gerald Watelet is a multi-talented interior designer.

Having recently opened his new shop in Uccle, Gerald brings his experience in haute couture and cookery to the table.

Visitors of IIDE 2019 have discovered some of his new lamp designs and exquisite rugs as a cacophony of texture and colour.

Gerald has collaborated with Houlès, Maison Brazet, Atelier Louise Pace/ Pierre Frey, Jim Thompson from Kafuji, Tagoli and Tiger Lily for this Salon 4 at IIDE.

Gerald Watelet
885 Chaussée de Waterloo, B-1180 Brussels
www.geraldwatelet.be
T +32 (0)2 646 06 12

Photography:
Andreas von Einsiedel

Salons 5 & 6

Guimar Urbina Interiors

Guimar Urbina
Photography: Andreas von Einsiedel

Guimar Urbina Interiors: a boutique experience

Guimar Urbina Interiors provide a boutique experience that goes beyond space planning and furniture selection.
Working internationally, Guimar takes personal pride in sourcing from her European contacts. She is pleased to have been introduced to the brand GHYCZY through the salon IIDE, including iconic pieces from the GHYCZY collection into her scheme.
GHYCZY have developed a headboard with side tables, launched at salon IIDE, shown with a super comfy Hästens bed from Sweden.

It has also been a pleasure working with Kinetura (pages 120-125), whom she discovered in Milan as remarkably talented Belgian lighting designers. Seeped in heritage, Guimar Urbina Interiors has taken a touch of Europe back to the United States to include in their international design schemes. Guimar has also collaborated with Technogym for the gym equipment in her Salons 5&6.

Guimar Urbina Interiors
444 Brickell Avenue, Suite 805, Miami, FL 33131
T +1 786 762 2675
www.guimarurbinainteriors.com
info@guimarurbinainteriors.com

Barbara Van Biervliet and Xaveer Claerhout, founders of Kinetura

Kinetura: Modulating light amplified by a poetic transformation

Kinetura is a Belgian company creating state-of-the-art lighting objects with a patented concept, combining light modulation with transformation of the shape.

Xaveer Claerhout, architect and master in art history and Barbara Van Biervliet, civil engineer-architect are the founders and inspiring source of Kinetura.

Some of their work has been acquired in the permanent collection of Musée du Centre Pompidou in Paris. Certain Kinetura designs also received international design awards such as the IF award, reddot Award and the German Design Award.

Objects and spaces transform in a silent and nearly imperceptible way into contrasting shapes with different functionality and expression, as if an organic, natural dimension were involved.

Focus of today's lighting is put on sustainable lighting and control systems, however, something is missing … Kinetura creates this missing link: lighting that physically transforms and adapts according to your needs of the moment. Dynamic lighting in the real meaning of the word, not only changing intensity, but also shape, functionality and atmosphere.

Kinetura
Nijverheidsweg 26, B-9820 Merelbeke
T +32 (0)50 50 01 50
www.kinetura.com
info@kinetura.com

Technogym: spreading the Wellness Lifestyle

For more than 35 years, Technogym has been helping people live healthier and happier.
Their mission is to spread the Wellness Lifestyle, engaging physical activity, correct nutrition and a positive mindset.

Their philosophy is to combine good design, attention to detail and the elegance of the product to complement your interior design and create a space that enhances your physical and mental balance.
Home wellness creates the best training and sports experience within the space that's most dear to us: our home.
Innovation, technology and design are features shared by all Personal products. Born out of the collaboration between Technogym and Antonio Citterio's studio Personal products are true design masterpiece created with refined materials processed with made in Italy craftsmanship.
Personal line features treadmills and other cardio equipment such as Run Personal, Recline Personal and Cross Personal. Kinesis Personal with its Vision and Heritage versions is the ideal solution for functional training. In closing strength is well represented by Power Personal.

Technogym Village
Via Calcinaro 2861 Cesena
www.technogym.com

Technogym Benelux
Ikaroslaan 25, B-1930 Zaventem
T +32 (0)2 720 86 33

Photography:
Andreas von Einsiedel

Salon 7

Benedetti Interieur with Evolution21

Vital Celen, CEO of Benedetti Interieur

Benedetti Interieur: master in decoration

Talent, a sense of beauty and perfection, craftsmanship, experience, a beautiful showroom with more than 10,000 fabrics, an own studio with skilled personnel and its own placement service have ensured that Benedetti Interieur has become a decoration master after forty years.

In our creations we love to work with style combinations and materials. Living spaces have to live, they need to be more than only being beautiful on a picture ... a bit of humour, some colours and a twist of glamour.

For many years we are striving for perfection and high quality craftsmanship. In our own workshop, unique in Belgium, we can make every fabric into a curtain of your dreams.

Until a few years ago, Benedetti Interieur mainly focused on window decoration, but that changed recently: at the request of the customers, complete interiors are also arranged by the team of interior designers at Benedetti.

Benedetti Interieur
Nijverheidsstraat 1, B-2235 Hulshout
www.benedetti.be
info@benedetti.be
T +32 (0)15 22 27 53

Karine Bonjean, CEO of Evolution21

Evolution21: tradition and innovation

Evolution21 has a solid reputation at an international level as an excellent producer of luxury products in the field of contemporary furniture design and as a representative of a classic-modern lifestyle in residential and hospitality projects.
Evolution21 today permanently melds tradition and innovation: the skills of talented artisan are employed to finish a product created by modern technologies, while the intelligence of the hands balances industrial precision with sensitivity and emotion. This high degree of know-how is constantly improved by the intensive research on materials and technological solutions thus enhancing the value of impeccable details. The commitment to excellence involves all the company.

Evolution21 has been providing its customers with quality furniture and textiles for a long time, making the company trustworthy regarding excellence and professionalism. The furniture and textiles are all handcrafted, reflecting Evolution21's regard towards customer satisfaction and luxury.

Evolution21 is known for its high-end textiles, leathers and furniture. With decades of experience, Karine Bonjean brings her creativity all across the world. She focuses towards warm and harmonious colors, to bring out a radiant and hospitable design for her customers.
The deepest roots of this long-lasting, successful collaboration in terms of the results it has given lie in the deep harmony that binds Karine Bonjean to Evolution21. Her cultural background, professional experience and sensitivity found fertile ground in a company that translated the designer's insights into finished projects.

Evolution21
Wayenborgstraat 24, B-2800 Mechelen
www.kb-evolution21.com
T +32 (0)15 31 33 63

Photography:
Jente Willems

Photography :
Gilles Piat - Studio Tekhné

Salon 8

LDécoration Internationale

Works of art chosen by Louise-Marie Hubert:

Left: Artwork *Factory in Mountain* by Christian Hidaka, Courtesy of the artist and Michel Rein, Paris/Brussels.
Sculpture *La Banquise #11* by Sophie Whettnall, Courtesy of the artist and Michel Rein, Paris/Brussels.
Chandelier *Perle Blanche* by Coup-de-foudre.

Right: A soft and cozy atmosphere created with the canvases of Jean Duruisseau, accompanied by an exclusive creation of a rug by Louise-Marie Hubert made by Braquenié.
Table custom designed by Laurence Glorieux, sheathed Braquenié fabric and Houlès piping.
New York chaise longue Pierre Frey, Houlès piping.
Christiane Löhr's Big Seed Cloud artwork, courtesy of the artist and the Bernier / Eliades gallery, Athens-Brussels.

Laurence Glorieux and Louise-Marie Hubert

Photography:
Andreas von Einsiedel

LDécoration Internationale: each project is unique…

Laurence Glorieux, interior designer, founder of LDécoration Internationale, builds bridges between now and then to create unique, "sur mesure" and high-end interiors. Excelling in assembling colours, textures, furnitures, fabrics, artworks and accessories, she works in collaboration with chosen artisans, suppliers, artists and savoir-faire. From historical monuments to private interiors, from architectural detail to the teaspoon, from north of Europe to the United States, LDécoration manages projects from A to Z. Along with Laurence, Louise-Marie Hubert, art advisor, Maité Goelhen, architect, and Marion Segard, interior designer, form a complementary team.
Each project is unique. With sensitivity and generosity, Laurence listens to each one's individuality and reveals the character of each place. Appreciating colours, and beautiful materials, she's an incomparable assembler.

The IIDE Room (pages 136-139)

As the season goes by and the snow melts
Flowers and colours emerge.
Will it stay?
Beauty came from our mother earth,
Soft colours, materials and light
To create this atmosphere.

L Décoration internationale
www.ldecoration.com

47 rue Saint Brice
B - 7500 Tournai
M +32 (0)479 59 64 98

Photography :
Gilles Piat – Studio Tekhné

For this iconic pâtisserie for more than four generations, LDécoration has built bridges between heritage and contemporary expressions.
Counter designed by Laurence Glorieux decorated with an exclusive creation by the mosaic artist Mathilde Jonquière.
Soft wall painting created for the place and molding enhanced with gold leaf.
Lighting in collaboration with Nuans.

Photography portrait Catherine Nyssen:
Cedric Paquet

Catherine Nyssen: Mastery and accuracy

Catherine Nyssen executes custom-made textile projects and creates unique pieces for extraordinary interiors. Her work is characterised by a combination of materials and artisanship to produce a unique and lasting result. Each fabric is painstakingly crafted to bring out all of its distinctive features and to skilfully yield the desired effect. Hand-finished, rough and sheer linen, wool, silk and trimmings combine and come together with mastery and precision.

The work of Catherine Nyssen's finishes translates into creations stripped bare or rich decorations adorned with braids, fringes and cords. For the Salon IIDE, C. Nyssen worked alongside Jean Duruisseau for the finish of the sections and cushions in plaster. She designed and worked on the Prelle fabric, applying Houlès trimmings.

Catherine Nyssen
Hookstrasse 56A
B-4700 Eupen
T +32 (0)87 33 58 56 M +32 (0)498 59 07 61
www.catherinenyssen.be cn@catherinenyssen.be
#ateliercatherinenyssen
Showroom Brussels: Oud Korenhuis 33, B-1000 Brussels

Photography :
Gilles Piat - Studio Tekhné

Houlès: worldwide recognition

Houlès is a French family owned company with worldwide recognition, extending from Paris to New York, Moscow to Dubai ...
In 1928, Félix and his son André Houlès established the parent company in the Faubourg Saint-Antoine area, traditional district for upholsterers, interior designers and architects. In the thirties, Suzanne and Pierre Houlès will turn this French family business into a company with international allure. Today, the company is managed with great passion and enthusiasm by their son, Philippe Houlès. Creator and designer of trimmings, hardware and fabrics collections, Houlès also sells upholstery supplies and accessories. Its clients are decoration stores, upholsterers, architects, interior designers and design offices, working on high-end residential projects (private homes and town houses), as well as contract projects (restaurants, luxury hotels...) and public projects (museums, theatres...).
Houlès creations are often selected for the decoration of palaces and castles like le Château de Versailles or Presidential Residences in France and abroad. The company also participates in many restoration works of prestigious historical monuments like the Bolshoi Theatre in Moscow. Over the years, thanks to its high-quality designs and service, Houlès has gained worldwide appeal. With its subsidiaries in Great-Britain, in the United States, in Italy, in Germany and thanks to its broad network of commercial agents and distributors, Houlès is nowadays established in more than 160 countries, with 4 showrooms : Paris, Dubaï, New-York, London. Houlès participates also to several great international fairs like Paris Deco Off, Bel etage, Madrid Intergift, Heimtex Switzerland, München Stoff Frühling or London design week. With regular new high-end creations based on historical know-how and decoration trends, a strong presence worldwide, the story of Houlès has continued with passion and ambition for 91 years.

Houlès Paris
13 Rue du Mail
FR-75002 Paris
T +33 (0)1 83 79 06 00
www.houles.com

Fabienne Duesberg
Houlès Belgique – Luxembourg
Rue du Petit Bois 3
B - 4500 Tihange
T +32 (0)477 35 55 95

Photography:
Steffy Stroobant

Photography:
Gilles Piat – Studio Tekhné

Jean Duruisseau: abstract artworks

Jean Duruisseau's abstract artworks communicate directly and with great emotional power. His Nomad installations and Monotype paintings tend to have a mesmerizing effect on the viewer. They free the viewer's mind from the dominance of reality and enable emotional and intuitive associations. Duruisseau paints with mineral pigments on custom woven Belgian linen.

JDR's Résidence des Artistes, in Tournai (Belgium), is an inspiring place and encouraging environment for the artists to experiment, create and interact. The co-working itself is a rich experience that allows common contribution towards creation, technique development and art renewal. The artists can share their works and stories with the public in the JDR art galleries in Tournai and Courtrai.

Jean Duruisseau made his mark in the interior design world by creating atmospheres with exclusive and unique artisanal floor and wall finishes. He has worked for private clients, as well in commercial projects, in places like Saint-Tropez, Prague, Andermatt, Paris, Munich and San Diego.

Jean Duruisseau
Avenue van Cutsem 20, B- 7500 Tournai (Belgium)
4 rue Grangevieille, FR- 43000 Le Puy en Velay (France)
www.jeanduruisseau.be
info@jeanduruisseau.be
Pieces on view and for sale at Amelie, Maison d'Art in FR-75009 Paris (8 rue Clauzel) and at Odilon Creations (Oud Korenhuis 33, B-1000 Brussels)

Photography:
Lenzer - Peter Verplancke

Coup-de-foudre: exclusive light objects

Coup-de-foudre are Goedel Vermandere and Jan Arickx.

We think of it as a story that started with an uprooting and which, over time and with plenty of plot twists, has evolved, from a temporary balance and upheavals to unity.

We have gradually established our roots, somewhere between life and work, between techniques and intuition, as business owners and artists, on the cusp between the studio and the client, between knowing and searching. Search for us and you'll find us, somewhere in the middle among all these contrasts.

Coup-de-foudre
Gentsestraat 17
B- 8500 Kortrijk
www.coup-de-foudre.be
M Goedel +32 (0)474 24 25 14
M Jan +32 (0)473 82 23 11
info@coup-de-foudre.be

Permanent exposition of Coup-de-foudre at Dirk Cousaert
Stationsstraat 160 , B-9690 Kluisbergen
www.dirkcousaert.be
Showroom Brussels
Oud Korenhuis 33, B-1000 Brussels

Misia:
sophisticated simplicity and modern elegance

With an increasingly international reputation, Casamance Group is an established, major player in the edition and distribution of fabrics, wallpapers, wallcoverings and trimmings ; bringing a new perspective to the world of decoration and to French-style elegance.

Today the Casamance Group brings together three brands, CASAMANCE, CAMENGO and MISIA, who with its twenty years of experience have allowed to create, grow and mature. Each of the three brands is independent and has its own story.

MISIA, created in 2014, is a showcase, seductive, playing with the rules of luxury. Searching for the freedom, audacity and glamour of the 1920s, the brand takes its inspirations from this decade of excesses, reinterpreted in an irrefutably modern way.

PARIS
13 rue du Mail, FR-75002 Paris
+33 9 83 05 91 13
showroom.paris@casamance.com

LONDON - CASAMANCE AT COLONY SHOWROOM
Design Centre Chelsea Harbour - 2nd Floor,
Dome Centre
+44 207 351 1299
showroom.uk@casamance.com

CULEMBORG
Randweg 20, 4104 AC Culemborg
+31 90000 401 616
showroom.nl@casamance.com

www.misia-paris.com
r.goure@texdecor.com

Furniture by Dominique Rigo in the house created by architect Marc Corbiau

Photography: Jo Pauwels

Dominique Rigo: contemporary interiors since 1974

A trained architect, Dominique Rigo quickly became passionate about the revolution in interior and furniture design in the early 1970s.

He has since contributed not only to the blossoming of modern design in Belgium but also to the success of the country's contemporary style in interior architecture.
His talent has manifested itself above all through his successive Brussels-based commercial addresses and contemporary interior design projects since 1974.

Dominique Rigo has always preferred a modernity which chooses comfort and functionality above the "trendy", the "way out" and the ridiculous. Function, form, comfort, quality and durability are still the overriding priorities in all the company's interior design projects ...from Brussels to Liège, from Geneva to Genoa, from London to New York...

Today, the father and two daughters partnership runs an interior design business comprising a team of seven interior architects and 3 modern furniture showrooms providing the largest and most comprehensive selection of contemporary furniture in Brussels.
The "Rigo" style is contemporary, yet not minimalist, with a penchant for the Italian and Scandinavian designed furniture and the icons of 20th Century design.
Several designs have never left the selection as today they have become "design classics"! Second daughter, Charlotte Rigo, joined the company straight after graduating in interior design in 1995. She has added a new dynamic to the company and her fresh approach to interior design projects is reflected in the evolution of the selection and presentation of products. Youngest daughter, Mélanie Rigo, joined in 2012 and oversees the company's image and communication.

Dominique Rigo
Rue de Stalle 210, B-1180 Uccle
T +32 (0)2 649 95 94

Other Dominique Rigo showrooms:
Cassina, avenue Louise 154, B-1050 Brussels
Vitrapoint Bruxelles, avenue Louise 154, B-1050 Brussels

www.dominiquerigo.be

Photography:
Pieter Huybrechts

Aristide: innovative fabrics and rugs

Welcome to the Aristide universe, a Belgium editor of furniture and decoration fabrics with accompanying carpets.

Aristide is an important player in the European interior design scene where they work together with interior and project designers, curtain studios, upholsterers and furniture manufacturers.

Aristide believes that good design should at all times reflect purpose and function, so they bring innovative, stylish basics with an original twist.

Aristide has supplied the beautiful rugs and fabrics in the IIDE Salons 5&6 (Guimar Urbina Interiors).

ARISTIDE nv
Nachtegaalstraat 109, B-2550 Kontich
T +32 (0)3 457 99 11
www.aristide.be
design@aristide.be

Postal address Aristide Netherlands: Nevelgaarde 40, NL-3436 ZZ Nieuwegein

Acknowledgements

The publisher wishes to thank Fleur Ross for her remarkable organizational talent, running each event from 1982 (the first BIDE) until the IIDE in Brussels in 2018 & 2019 single handed.
Fleur has also been a great help in the preparation of this book and in assembling the archives from her BIDE exhibitions in London (1982-1997).

We also wish to thank all participants to the BIDE exhibitions in London and the IIDE in Brussels for their support.

Publisher

Beta-Plus Publishing
avenue Louise 367
B-1050 Brussels
www.betaplus.com
info@betaplus.com

Graphic Design

Oil in Water, Brussels